Rap[illegible]

Programming

GUI Creation, Django Web Server,

Game Programming, and Stock Analysis

Rapid Python Programming

William C. Gunnells

GUI Creation, Django Web Server, Game Programming, and Stock Analysis

Printed by CreateSpace, An Amazon.com Company

1st Edition

Notice of Liability

Trademarks

Editor

For copy editing and instructor-led training contact Rachel Gunnells via email rachelgunnells@icloud.com

Contact

For information about buying this title in bulk quantities, or for special sales opportunities, please contact author via info@rapidpythonprogramming.com or visit us on the web at http://www.rapidpythonprogramming.com

ISBN-13: 978-1541043084

ISBN-10: 1541043081

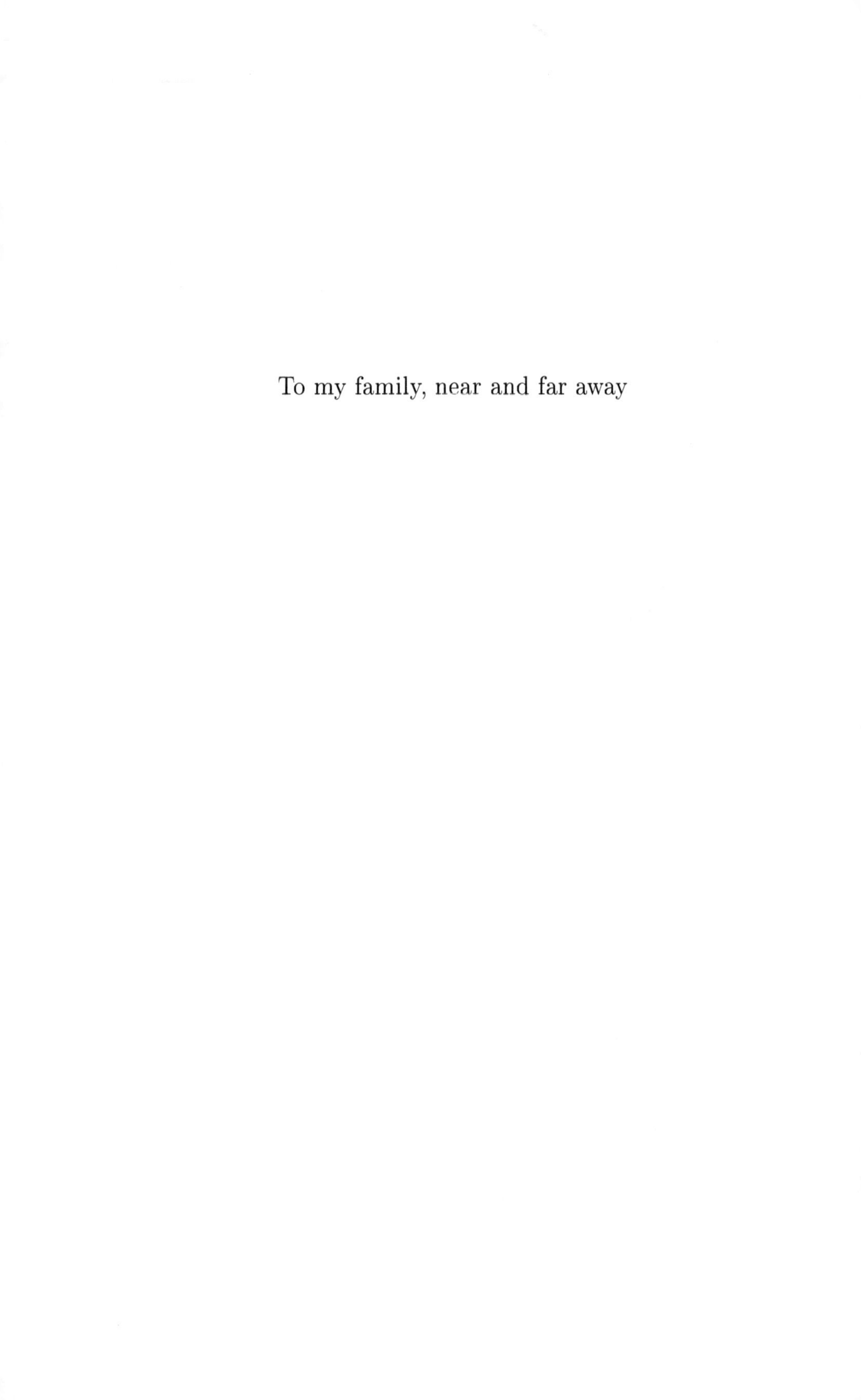

To my family, near and far away

Contents

List of Tables

List of Figures

Part I.

Beginning

Part 1

-Python the fast way

Preface

Preface

Python is one of the few programming languages that is not only easy to learn but also very powerful. Most books on programming focus on the skill level of the reader rather then the topic for which the reader picked the book. I got the idea to write this book after reading "Programming - Principles and Practice Using C++ written by Bjarne Stroustrup the creator of C++ programming language. While everything here will be presented differently, the philosophy of programming, learning and the methods he presented is what influenced me the most.

Programs by nature evolve towards complexity and most languages foster the ability to design in a structured way even if the language is not a structured programming language. Python supports multi-paradigms (such as object oriented, imperative, and functional). The design of Python leans towards a clean modular style with everything loosely considered an object.

Once you start programming with python, you won't want to use other languages. You may even find yourself converting code written in other languages to python. Python is very fast. You can compile your code into Byte-compiled files or PYC files. These pre-compiled binaries execute quickly. Conveniently Byte-compiled files that are created by the python interpreter automatically and can be further extended with other python modules. If you decide to use python for science, or gaming, and you need more speed, you can further extend python with the "C" language. The flexible features of python make it an excellent choice for beginners and experts. Most important, programming with python is fun.

For the more experienced developer, python can be learned on a one page cheat sheet. Taking into account the range of skill levels and learning styles, my idea was to provide just enough examples to learn the language then introduce the reader to the fun tools. The reality is that the beginner will learn just enough to program then comb through endless "Google" pages to understand tasks such as: parsing large files, working with a database, doing network programming, creating a graphical interface, designing a website, developing a game, or modeling and stock market analysis. My goal is to teach the student just enough that they feel confident jumping right into the fun stuff.

Here are some of the highlights:

EasyGUI

This is a wonderful chapter for newbies, providing you a graphical environment in which to program

Tkinter

Now that the reader has cut their teeth on the basics of EasyGUI, it's only a few more steps to writing Tkinter applications without EasyGUI templates.

WxWidgests

WxWidgets is one of the most popular cross platform GUI libraries available. It is used by a lot of popular high level programming languages.

Network Programming

This chapter explains how to use sockets, and build client and server applications.

SQLite

Chapter 19. Is about SQlite, a very lightweight SQL server, that has many advantages over a traditional SQL server. It's really easy to learn and easy for Python to connect to.

CGI

Often enough Web application developers run into certain limitations. The client might have a server co-located with a provider that only supports PHP and CGI. This chapter explains how to utilize python with CGI.

WSGI

Web Server Gateway Interface. It is a specification for web servers and application servers to communicate with web applications.

Pygame

This chapter is about the Pygame library, how to utilize it, a short tutorial, examples, and options for deployment.

How to use this book

Learning python can be achieved relatively quickly in 6 chapters at the most. I explain everything in the simple terms and provide exercises. To get the most use out of this book it's recommended that you type everything out. There is no substitute for learning how to deal with typos than the experience of troubleshooting your own code.

Conventions

The python code snippets are italicized with a smaller font. Most of the results or corresponding output are provided in the same format. Some of the code might be truncated. Ellipses or comments similar to the following (#...) indicate regions where code exists that isn't essential for expressing a point.

Code and Errata

It's useful to view examples in this book as whole programs without interleaved prose. You can find the source code for all code snippets in this book on our website:

http://www.rapidpythonprogramming.com.

Corrections for any errors found in the book can be found on the website.

Acknowledgments

Acknowledgments

This book would not have been possible without the guidance and support of many people in my life.

Thanks to my friends who have always encouraged me through trials and tribulations navigating the fiercely competitive computer technology industry. They always encouraged me to remember to stay focused and believe in myself.

Thanks to Dennis Feick who had enduring faith in my family during some of the worst economic times as a programmer these last 7 years.

Thanks to the wonderful programmers I've known and worked with: Dan White and Daniel Yount have both been helpful and inspirational in this matter. I appreciate their tutelage over the years. It was a pleasure working with them.

Thanks to my family, Rachel, Olaf, and Mckinzie who stood by me and endured the late hours of work, overtime, and sacrifices made as a writer while working multiple jobs.

About the Author

Author

William Gunnells has been building computers since he was 10 years old. While hardware is his passion he loves to exploit the various hardware features through software. Hardware has changed so much in the last 30 years. The market wants smaller, faster, better. It's the same with software. Python is smaller, faster, and better. With more than 25 years as a programmer, network engineer, and security engineer. He designs and engineers from scratch full service solutions using open source tools to enterprise standards for the target market. His diverse background is as follows:

Network Penetration

Working knowledge of buffer overflows, race conditions, protocol hijacking, replay attacks, stealth attacks, network sniffing, password cracking, denial of service, spoofing, covert channels, network tunneling, connection bouncing, system call hijacking and "Userland rootkits". Concentrated knowledge on TCP/IP and network attack scenarios.

Programming

He is proficient in shell scripting (bash, CSH), C, Perl, Python, PHP, GNU debugger and build tools (Automake, Autoconf, Libtool), Version Control (CVS, RCS), Perforce, GIT, and SVN on large-scale development projects. Extensive experience at utilization of both asymmetric and symmetric ciphers.

He has developed custom code for OpenBSD and Linux Loadable Kernel Modules (LKM). Experience using Queue, Libnet, Libpcap, Pthreads and Ncurses API's. Extensive research in theory and practical implementation of network protocols: [R]ARP, DNS, IPv4 IPv6, ICMP, GMP, OSPF, RIP, TCP, UDP, and SNMP. Vast experience in web development (CMF, CRM, ERP), web languages, HTML, Python, PHP, XML, CSS, MySQL, Postgres, Gadfly, and SQLite.

Network Security and Forensics Investigation:

Extensive experience with AIX, BSD(i), IRIX, HPUX, Linux, SCO, Solaris, Snort Intrusion Detection Systems. Configuration and Management of Checkpoint, IPF, OpenBSD PF, IPtables, Cisco (ASA, ASAFWSM, ASASM) and Raptor Firewalls. He has extensive technical writing experience, documenting many Operating Systems in a threatened scenario, extensive forensics analysis and assessment experience of enterprise environments, investigative procedures and documentation.

- Website Backend Development
- Responsive Web Tool Development
- Content Management Systems
- WordPress Theme Integration
- Drupal Theme Integration
- Mobile Platform Development
- Usability Testing
- Django Python Integration
- Python Development
- Content Management Framework Creation
- Analytics
- Social Media

- Embedded Systems Development
- ADC Systems Development

In his spare time he writes web applications for small contracts, geeks out on new technologies, and designs gambling software.

1. Introduction

1.1. Introduction

The Python programming community is rapidly growing. More people are either migrating to python or choosing it as their first high level programming language. It's multiple programming paradigms feature make it an easier first language to learn, because it frees you from focusing on the language itself, and more on problem solving. Python is highly portable for multiple operating systems, including embedded systems. It's also "Open Source" and can be distributed freely.

This book can be used for the experienced programmer, or absolute beginner. The complexity of the language gradually progresses, but the concepts will remain simple and easy to understand. Readers are not restricted to any previous specific concept. All concepts and examples can be easily modified and re-used. You will be able to play with the advanced features of python quickly.

The job market is putting a higher demand for fast turnaround on development for new products. It's also becoming a heavy hitter in the game market for its use throughout the game development cycle such as rendering, parsing, statistics and core development. Python can be easily extended using C/C++ for speed and performance. It's used extensively in Academia for Science, Math, Engineering, simulations, and other computation experiments. Python's greatest selling point is the vast libraries of pre-written tools. Below is a highlight of tools which comprises approximately 10% of what actually exists.

- **Integrated Development Environments** - Boa Constructor, a cross-platform IDE for Python - EasyEclipse, an open source IDE for Python and other languages.
- **Applications** - BitTorrent original client, as well as other derivatives - Gajim, an Instant Message client - Resolver One, a spreadsheet.
- **Web Applications** - A feed Aggregator (Planet), a user-friendly Content Management System (Plone), a bug tracking system (Roundup).
- **Video games** - Civilization 4 uses python for most of its tasks, Eve "online" uses Stackless Python. PyGame has tons of games written in pure python.
- **Web frameworks** - CherryPy an object-oriented web application server and framework, Django an MVC (Model, View, Controller) web framework, Zope is an application server commonly used to build content management systems.
- **Graphics frameworks** - Pygame has python bindings for Simple DirectMedia Layer (SDL), Pyglet is a cross-platform windowing and multimedia library for Python, PIL (Python Imaging Library) a module for working with images, Soya 3D is a high-level 3D game engine for Python.
- **GUI frameworks** - PyGTK is a popular cross-platform GUI library using GTK+, PyQt is another cross-platform GUI library using Qt, wxPython is a port of wxWidgets and a cross-platform GUI library for Python.
- **Scientific packages** - BioPython, a Python molecular biology suite. SciPy is a library of scientific and numerical routines.
- **Mathematical libraries** - matplotlib, an extension providing MATLAB-like plotting and mathematical functions. NumPy is a language extension that adds support for large and fast, multi-dimensional arrays and matrices.

- **Additional development packages** - Cheetah, a Python-powered template engine and code-generation tool, mod python is an Apache module allowing direct integration of Python scripts with the Apache web server, Twisted is a networking framework for Python
- **Embedded as a scripting language** - GIMP- (Graphics Image Manipulation Program) , Blender, 3d graphics program , Inkscape is a Graphics program , Poser is a 3D rendering and animation software program that uses PoserPython tool-set.
- **Commercial uses** - Google uses Python for many tasks including the Backends of web App's, Maya is a professional 3D modeler, NASA is using Python to implement a CAD/CAE/PDM repository and model management, integration, and transformation system.
- **Python implementations** - IronPython, Python for .NET and Mono platforms - Jython, Python coded in Java - Stackless Python, Python with co-routines.

What makes this book unique is the transition from beginner to intermediate programming. The transition will occur several times throughout the book, when introducing a new topic such as web applications and GUI. You will revisit beginning aspects of programming to simplify learning a new module, instead of assuming you are already proficient in the previous techniques discussed. Most importantly you will be instructed in the ability to convert code to other programming styles and technique; this will make it easy to adopt any style or method when re-using reusable code. Python also has an enhancement program known as PEP (Python Enhancement Program), which contains an index of potential proposals to further enhance the python programming language. Python is evolving towards 3.x which includes minor changes with regards to backwards compatibility. A chapter at the end of the book will be devoted to compatibility changes and migration.

1.1.1. History

Python was created in the late 1980s by Guido van Rossum at CWI in the Netherlands and was a successor to the ABC programming language. Python was re-designed to be a multi-paradigm programming language making it possible for programmers to adopt multiple styles of programming such as object-oriented programming, structured, functional, aspect-oriented programming and meta programming.

1.1.2. Installation

It is highly recommended that you use Linux as your primary platform to learn and use python. However you are not restricted. Nearly everything can be done in Microsoft Windows™ or Apple Macintosh™ with few troubles.

1.1.3. Windows

Visit http://www.python.org/download and you will find an installer for windows. Select all installation components.

If you wish to use Python in Microsoft Windows™ on the command line, then you need to set the PATH variable appropriately.

For Windows™ 2000, XP, 2003, Vista, 2008, etc... click on Control Panel -> System -> Advanced -> Environment variables. Click on the variable named PATH in the "System Variables" section, then select:

Edit and add; C:\Python27 to the end of the line.

Please choose proper directory name. For instance: it could be C:\Python2.7x

1.1.4. Linux

Most Linux distributions come with Python installed by default. However you may need to install additional packages such as the documentation. For example, Knoppix or Debian run the following:

```
sudo apt-get install python27-doc
```

By selecting the defaults, you will have installed python core files including documentation, such as, interactive help and manual pages.

You can verify the version of python via the command line using "python -V" as shown below.

```
$ python -V
Python 2.7.9
```

1.1.5. Editors

Choosing an editor can be very crucial for the successful development of your scripts. You have to be completely comfortable with your editor and have full knowledge of how it writes files. For instance, scripts written on Microsoft Windows™ Notepad can have several issues when you port the files to a Linux or BSD operating system. Those files might have carriage return issues Control-M (^M) on each statement. You would have to manually remove them on each statement or do a file wide search and replace which can be tricky because you need an escape code to find it. The escape code is (x0D) or (\x0D). However you can avoid these issues by using a compatible editor.

1.1.6. Case Sensitive

You might have noticed Microsoft Windows™ is not case sensitive. However, on a Unix variant operating system or Linux, you will need to be more specific when executing scripts. For example, typing "python" at the command prompt would list the following:

Note: To exit out of the interpreter press "Ctrl-D" followed by enter or type "exit()".

```
$ python
Python 2.7.6 (default, Mar 22 2014, 22:59:56)
[GCC 4.8.2] on linux2
Type "help", "copyright", "credits" or "license" for more information.
>>>
```

Uppercase Python would reveal an error as follows:

```
$ Python -bash: Python: command not found
```

If you are using python in iOS, Apple accepts the uppercase "Python", and you will not see an error.

1.1.7. Additional Packages

You will learn how to download the following packages in later chapters as you need them:

- **python-doc** - Documentation for the high-level object-oriented-programming.
- **python-docutils** - Utilities for the documentation of Python.
- **python2.7-doc** - Documentation for the high-level object-oriented language.
- **python-django** - A high-level Python Web framework python-gtk2 - Python bindings for the GTK+ widget sets.
- **python-sqlite** - Python interface to SQLite 2 (currently included as of 2.6).

- **python-tk** - Tkinter - Writing Tk applications with Python python-pygame, and writing game applications using Python2.7x.
- **python-wxWidgets** – Writing Wx applications with Python.
- **zope3** – Web application framework.

1.1.8. Versions

At the beginning of this project all applications were compiled using python version 2.7. Before completion of this project all applications were compiled and tested with Python version 2.8. The code will work in Python 3.x with minor changes such as: print statement. Almost everything here is backwards compatible and will translate easily into Python 3 if you familiarize yourself with the minor syntactical changes. Don't let the version of python distract you. The changes are often very minor. See the two following examples below:

- Python 2.2x is: print variable.
- Python 3.x is: print(variable)

* Please visit http://www.wiki.python.org/moin/Python2orPython3

1.1.9. Installation and Configuration

It is highly recommended that you choose an Operating System that you are proficient using. It is assumed that you have a clear understanding of your Operating System and how to execute programs via command line.

1.1.10. Python Interactive Prompt

For Microsoft Windows™users, Python interactive interpreter can be executed via the DOS prompt or through the "IDLE". (Interactive Development Environment) program.

To start the interactive interpreter enter "python" at the command or shell prompt in Windows or xterm in Linux or Terminal in iOS.

The following information should appear:

knoppix@Microknoppix:~$ ***python***
Python 2.5.2 (r252:60911, Jan 4 2009, 17:40:26)[GCC 4.3.2]
on linux2 Type "help", "copyright", "credits" or "license"
for more information.
>>>

You can immediately begin typing your program

```
>>> print 'I am learning python'
I am learning python
>>>
```

Please note that python is case sensitive. *Print* will give you an invalid syntax error.

```
>>> Print 'hello'
  File "<stdin>", line 1

    Print 'hello'
                ^

SyntaxError: invalid syntax
>>>
```

To exit out of the interpreter press "Ctrl-D" followed by enter or type "exit()".

1.1.11. Making a Python Script

You can create a script using an editor. If you are using Microsoft Windows™ I suggest you use IDLE or editpad to create your script. You may need to download editpad from: http://www.editpadpro.com. If you are using Linux, I suggest using VIM as your editor or Sublime for iOS. Open your editor, create a new file and type the following into the editor:

```
print 'I am learning python'
```

Save the file as first.py

Once the file is saved you can type the following on the command line or terminal:

```
knoppix@Microknoppix:~$ python first.py
I am learning python
knoppix@Microknoppix:~$
```

A proper script would include the path to the interpreter, a description, the name of the file and other files that might be involved. The path to the interpreter is not needed while using python on a windows™ operating system.

```
#!/usr/bin/python
# program name first.py
print 'I am learning python'
```

Edit the file with the information in the figure above, then Save and Close the file. If you are on a Linux system, you will need to change the file permissions to make it an executable program.

```
knoppix@Microknoppix:~$ chmod a+x fist.py
```

You can then execute the program as follows:

```
knoppix@Microknoppix:~$ ./first.py
I am learning python
knoppix@Microknoppix:~$
```

Notice the #! hash or number symbol and exclamation. It's known in Unix or Linux as "explode" and "bang" or "sha-bang" which is the key to execute the shell or interpreter. Anything after the first line is considered either code or comments. Comments are designated using the hash (#) symbol. On Windows™ the path to the Python interpreter will be, for example, c:\python27.x\python.exe. You can also omit (#!) on first line.

Python's built-in interpreter also has a nice interactive feature known as help(). To start the interactive interpreter enter "python" at the command or shell prompt:

```
knoppix@Microknoppix:~$ python
Python 2.5.2 (r252:60911, Jan 4 2009, 17:40:26) [GCC 4.3.2]
on
linux2 Type "help", "copyright", "credits" or "license"
for more information.
```

```
>>> help()
Welcome to Python 2.7! This is the online help utility.

If this is your first time using Python, you should definitely
check out the tutorial on the Internet at
http://www.python.org/doc/tut/.

Enter the name of any module, keyword, or topic to get help
on
writing Python programs and using Python modules. To quit
this help utility and return to the interpreter, just type "quit".

To get a list of available modules, keywords, or topics, type
"modules", "keywords", or "topics". Each module also comes
with a one-line summary of what it does; to list the modules
whose summaries contain a given word such as "spam", type
"modules spam".

help>
```

To exit out of help mode type '**q**' and it will put you back into the interpreter mode >>>. With this interactive help you can learn about almost anything in Python, for example:

```
>>> help('str')
```

Will print out the documentation for "str" or string.

To get a list of modules, or keywords, type *'**modules**'*. It will take a minute to compile but will provide a list of modules. If you wish to learn about a specific module, pick one of the two formats shown below.

```
>>> help('module-name') or
help> module-name.
```

1.1.12. Summary

In this chapter you have learned how to use the interactive interpreter, how to create and execute scripts, and how to activate the interactive help module.

1.1.13. Exercises

1. Go through the examples above using the interactive interpreter.
2. Create a script to print out a list of all modules and redirect that list to a file called "python-modules.txt".
3. Create another script to print the print module and redirect to file called "python-print.txt".

2. Strings - Operators - Conditions

2.0.14. Strings

- **Single Quotes**

You already wrote your first string **print 'I am learning python'**. Next, open up the command prompt or terminal and input the following string into the interpreter **print 'It's my python'**. You should receive an error. It's because of the extra single quote. Now try it with an escape key called the back slash (\): **print 'It\'s my python'**. If you need a back slash such as in 'the good \ the bad \ the ugly' just add an extra escape key (\\).

```
>>> print 'the good \\ the bad \\ the ugly'.
the good \ the bad \ the ugly
```

- **Double Quotes**

Your scripts might look a little better if you swap between single and double quotes as needed.

```
>>> print "It's your python"
It's your python
```

- **Triple Quotes** (''' or """)

Before we move into triple quotes keep in mind that you can also create a string like 'this'.

```
>>> 'this'
'this'
```

We can create the string but we really don't have to do anything with it. The interpreter will tell you what it is. Next enter the following into the interpreter. (Make sure to enter 3 single quotes before and after). Warning a double quote and single quote together will give a different error.

```
>>> '''line 1
... line 2'''
'line 1\nline 2'
```

Notice the (\n) for new line. Try it with print in front of it and it will put the string in two separate lines.

```
>>> print '''line 1
... line 2'''
line 1
line 2
```

If you enter "\n" the following string will be displayed on a new line..

```
>>> print 'I\ngo'
I
go
```

The results will be the same with >>>"""". Now a raw string with some slight changes. Try it at the interpreter.

```
>>> r'string'
'string'
>>> r'string\string2'
'string\\string2'
>>> r"string\string2"
'string\\string2'
>>> print r"string\string2"
string\string2
>>> r"""string\string2"""
'string\\string2'
>>> print r"""string\string2"""
string\string2
```

The last example is to show that you can test your expressions as your scripts progress towards complexity in the future. The string examples above will become more evident as you progress. In section 3.2.3 there is an example of printing a string, integer, or float in a print statement on the same line.

2.0.15. Variables and Assignment

Assignments must begin with either an (upper or lower case) letter or an underscore (_). A number can be used after the first letter or underscore. Here are some examples. Please try each one to get a feel for the effect.

```
>>> var1=1
>>> print var1
1
>>> a=2
>>> print a
2
>>> b,c=3,4
>>> print b,c
3 4
>>> s= 'string'
>>> print s
string
>>> s
'string'
```

2.0.16. Operators, Order, Indent

These are the most commonly used operators. The rest are listed in the appendix.

Table 2.1.: Common Operators

Operator	Name	Example
+	Plus	2+2 gives 4
-	Minus	4-2 gives 2
*	Multiplication	2*6 gives 12
/	Division	6/2 gives 12
%	Modulus	8%3 gives 2
<	Less than	8<4 gives false
>	Greater Than	8>4 gives true
<=	Less Than or equal	8<=4 gives false
>=	Greater Than or equal	8>=4 gives false
==	Equal	x=2; x==2 gives true
!=	not equal	x=2; x!=3 gives true
**	power	2**2 gives 4, 2**3 gives 8

Type in the following expressions:

```
>>> 8+8
16
>>> 8-4
4
>>> 4*2
8
>>> 8/2
4
>>> 2+3*8
26
>>> 2/3
0
>>> 2.0/3.0
0.66666666666666663
```

Notice that in the equation 2+3*8, multiplication comes before addition. You can change this around by using parenthesis (2+3)*8 gives 40. Also notice 2/3 gives 0. Since it's an integer it returns the appropriate integer. If you know that the expression yields a decimal place, then supply it to begin with, otherwise you will corrupt your output.

2.0.17. Pitfalls

You may have noticed with the above examples that you can run into many pitfalls. Truncation, and conversion are the primary causes of corruption. Always test your work first before deployment.

2.0.18. Integer Conversion

```
>>> number=1234
>>> int(number)
1234
>>> int(12.34)
12
>>> round(12.34)
12.0
>>>oct(number)
'02322'
>>> hex(number)
'0x4d2'
>>> print 2**256
115792089237316195423570985008687907853269984665640564039457584007913129639936
>>> x=1234567890
>>> y=3489493838
>>> x+y
4724061728L
>>> x*x
1524157875019052100L
>>> x*y
4308017044747661820L
```

As you can see, "python" supports large integers out of the box. However you might see the "L" statement as listed in above examples. This really depends on the operating system.

2.1. Conditions and Indentation

2.1.1. Flow Control if/else

help("if")

The if statement is used for conditional execution: Please DO NOT type the following.

```
if_stmt ::= "if" expression ":" suite
( "elif" expression ":" suite )*
["else" ":" suite]
```

2.1.2. For Loop

help("for")

The for statement is used to iterate over the elements of a sequence (such as a string, tuple or list) or other iterable object. The syntax is below:

```
for_stmt ::= "for" target_list "in" expression_list ": "
suite
["else" ":" suite]
```

2.1.3. While Loop

The while statement is used for repeated execution as long as an expression is true. Again, the syntax is below.

```
while_stmt ::= "while" expression ":" suite
["else" ":" suite]
```

2.1.4. Examples

Now we can learn a little about flow and conditions. You can utilize the interactive interpreter, but keep in mind that if you exit out early and connect back later, you will need to reinitialize x=3 again to test out the conditions. The preferred way would be to enter this into a file called "conditions.py". Using your favorite editor, run it using the following command: "python ./conditions.py".

Pay ATTENTION to indentation!

```
x=3
if x < 4:
    print "x is less then 4 x is ",x
if (x < 4 or x > 2):
    print "x is less then 4 and greater than 2, x=", x
if x == 1:
    print "Item 1 - true value", x
elif x == 2:
    print "Item 2 - true value", x
elif x == 3:
    print "Item 3 - true value", x
else:
    print "Default option if none listed", x
for i in [1,2,3,4,5,6,7,8,9,10]:
    print "Iteration #", i
for i in range(5):
    print i # note this prints up to 4
while (x< 10):
    print "The while iteration is.", x
    x=x+1
```

Indentation can be either a space or a tab. Whichever you choose will set the level for the rest of the script. After you run "conditions.py" feel free to edit it and change the values. You can remove the indentation and read the errors. With what you have learned you can compute just about any algorithm. Of course input functions, and methods would round out your knowledge and can be found in the next chapter.

2.1.5. Conditions and Indentation

You can utilize the interactive interpreter or continue to use your favorite editor. Enter the following data into a file called **"conditions.py"**.

Pay ATTENTION to indentation!

```
x=3
if x < 4:
    print "x is less then 4 x is ",x # notice the space (is
",x)
if (x < 4 or x > 2):
```

```
        print "x is less then 4 and greater then 2, x=", x #
notice (x=", x)
    if x == 1:
        print "Item 1 - true value", x
    elif x == 2:
        print "Item 2 - true value", x
    elif x == 3:
        print "Item 3 - true value", x
    else:
        print "Default option if none listed", x
```

The results are:

x is less then 4 x is 3
x is less then 4 and greater than 2, x= 3
Item 3 - true value 3

Standard iteration:

```
for i in [1,2,3,4,5]:
    print "Iteration #", i
```

results:

Iteration # 1
Iteration # 2
Iteration # 3
Iteration # 4
Iteration # 5

Iterate a range:

```
for i in range(5):
    print i # note this prints up to 4
```

results:

0
1
2
3
4

Notice that it went from 0 to 4. You can change where it starts by setting an additional parameter range(1,5) so it will start with 1 and end with 4.

```
while (x< 10):
    print "The while iteration is.", x
    x=x+1
```

Figure 2.1.: Formula Temperature

formula for Celsius to Fahrenheit $c * \frac{9}{5} + 32 = x$ python code for this would be as simple as (c*9/5+32)

The results are: **x** initialize as **3**

while iteration is. 3
while iteration is. 4
while iteration is. 5
while iteration is. 6
while iteration is. 7
while iteration is. 8
while iteration is. 9

Notice that indention is very important and can be either a space or tab. Whichever you choose first sets the key or level for the rest of the script. Please change some of the values in the "conditions.py" to get different results.

2.1.6. Summary

In this chapter you will have learned how strings work, and how to supply a number or string to a variable and operators. With what you have learned so far you can compute just about any algorithm. However things would be easier if functions (methods) are used. This will be discussed in later chapters.

2.1.7. Exercises

1. Go through the examples above using the interactive interpreter.
2. Write a program to calculate 20 degrees Celsius and convert to Fahrenheit.

3. Continue with previous exercise using variable 'c' calculate Celsius to Fahrenheit on one line and Fahrenheit to Celsius on another line.
4. Go through the examples above using the interactive interpreter.
5. Create a program to print out your name that has been assigned to a variable 's'.
6. Multiply your name by 5 and create a new line each time the name is printed out.
7. Continue with the previous exercise and assign the variable of 5 to x and multiply 's' by 'x'.
8. Go through the examples above using the interactive interpreter.
9. Print out a list of temperatures Celsius to Fahrenheit only using c=20, c=25, c=30, c=40.
10. If the temperature exceeds 90 F print (its hot) if temperate is lower then 70 F print (its cool) otherwise print (its just fine).

3. Input - Data structures, Modules

3.1. Input Function

3.1.1. input()

Create a file called 'input.py' with the following two lines below. Execute the program with 'python ./input.py' and input the number **'2'**. Next, run it again and input the letter **'d'**.

```
#input.py
x = input("Enter a number: ")
print "The square of number is", x*x
```

Results when running 'python input.py':

```
Enter a number: 2
The square of number is 4
```

Again type 'python input.py':

```
Enter a number: d
Traceback (most recent call last):
File "input.py", line 1, in <module>
  x = input("Enter a number: ")
File "<string>", line 1, in <module>
NameError: name 'd' is not defined
```

As you can see '**d**' is not defined and so it crashes! What if '**d**' was defined in the code? Create a new file with the following as save as 'input-hack.py'.

```
#input-hack.py
d=5
x = input("Enter a number: ")
print "The square of number is ", x*x
```

When you run the program you can now enter any number, and when you enter the letter 'd' it's already defined and should return 25. The 'input()' function is very dangerous, because it uses 'raw_input' and converts the data to a number using 'eval()'. Run the program again and type 2+2. It should return 16.

If you change the code from 'x*x' to 'x+x', and run the script again with 'raw_input()' like in the next example. The string of your choice will be duplicated twice. This is a warning to advise you not to use 'input()' as it can create inconsistencies in the results as well as an opportunity to hack the code.

3.1.2. raw_input()

Let's create another file 'rawinput.py'

```
#rawinput.py
x = raw_input("Enter a number or string: ")
print "you entered ", x
```

Please test the results and you will notice greater consistency. Further improvements can be made by reviewing the errors, substitute 'x' with 'x*x' and you will get an ('TypeError': can't multiply sequence by non-int of type ('str') when you enter a number.

3.1.2.1. Guess Program

```
#guess.py
number = 10
guess = int(raw_input('Enter a number between 1 & 20:
'))
if guess == number:
    print 'Congrats! Correct number is', number
elif guess < number:
    print 'No, try a little higher'
else:
    print 'No, try a little lower'
```

The guess program has 'raw_input' wrapped to an integer called 'int'. So the string is converted to an integer after you enter the number and hit return. If you change the 'raw_input()' to ***guess = raw_input("Enter an integer between 1 and 20: ')***. The 'if else' statement will try to process the string, and default to the last else statement.

You can wrap this code with a while statement as follows:

```
#whileguess.py
number=10
while True:
    guess = int(raw_input('Enter a number between 1 &
20: '))
    if guess == number:
        print 'Congrats! Correct number is', number
        break
    elif guess < number:
        print 'No, try a little higher'
    else:
        print 'No, try a little lower'
```

Notice I added the break statement if the value is true it exits out of the loop.

3.1.3. Declare a Function

The most common function to declare is a simple 'hello' statement.

```
#hello.py
def hello():
    print "Hello"
    return
hello()
```

You call the function with 'hello()'. A more practical function would be to

process the square of a number.

```
def square(x):
    return x*x
print square(2) # call the function
```

You can expand this function with 'raw_input'.

```
#inputfunction.py
def square(x):
    return x*x
x = int(raw_input("Enter a number "))
print "input without function ",x
print "input with function ",square(2)
```

This is also a mild example of local vs global where the square is local to

the function. The input is global.

3.1.4. Functions with Parameters

```
#function with parameter
#functionpar.py
def areaSquare(a,b):
    return a*b
print areaSquare(2,3)
z=4
y=2
print areaSquare(z,y)
```

3.1.5. Functions with Default Arguments

functions with default 'args':

```
#functionarg.py
def tableLeaf(a,b=5):
    return a*b
print tableLeaf(5,10)
print tableLeaf(5)
```

Here is another way to write this that might be easier for others to follow.

```
#functionarg.py
def tableLeaf(a,b=5):
    print "area of table:", a*b
tableLeaf(5,10)
tableLeaf(5)
```

Another example with input.

```
#functionarg-input.py
def tableLeaf(a,b=5):
    print "area of table:", a*b
x = int(raw_input("enter a number: "))
tableLeaf(x)
```

You can expand this by adding another 'raw_input' and assign it to 'y'. Then call 'tableLeaf(x,y)'.

3.2. Data Structures

3.2.1. help(list)

The features for list are extensive from counting items in the list to inserting, removing, appending and sorting. Roughly 50 attributes exist to manipulate a list.

```
#mylist.py
mylist = ['cpu', 'monitor', 'printer', 'keyboard', 'mouse']
print 'mylist contains the following:',
for i in mylist:
    print i
print "I have",len(mylist), 'items in mylist'
print "I am adding ink to mylist"
mylist.append('ink')
print "mylist append: ",mylist
mylist.sort()
print "mylist sorted: ",mylist
print "first item in mylist: ",mylist[0]
print "second item in mylist: ",mylist[1]
del mylist[1]
print "removed second item in mylist: ",mylist
```

3.2.2. help(tuple)

Tuples are similar to lists except they are immutable like strings. You would use them when you are sure that they will not change.

```
#mytuple.py
mytuple = ('pen', 'pencils', 'paper')
print 'mytuple contains: ',mytuple
print 'I have',len(mytuple), 'in mytuple'
drawer = ('ruler', 'paperclips', mytuple)
print 'mytuple and drawer contain: ',drawer
print 'first item in first tuple is : ',drawer[2][0]
```

3.2.3. Tuple in Print Statement

The following attributes "%s" for string "%d" for integer, and "%f" float which defaults to 6 decimal places.

```
#tupleprint.py
book = "Wheel of Time Dragon Reborn"
cost = 45.9
print 'This %s book is %d' % (book, cost)
print 'This %s book is %f' % (book, cost)
print 'This %s book is %6.4f' % (book, cost)
print 'This %s book is %6.2f' % (book, cost)
```

3.2.4. Dictionary

help('dict')

A dictionary is like an address book. This example will use an inventory system.

```
#inventory.py
inv = {'monitors': 'two', 'printers': 5, 'keyboards':3}
print inv["printers"]
inv['printers'] = 6
print inv['printers']
print inv
del inv['keyboards']
print inv
for i,j in inv.iteritems():
    print i, j
```

3.2.5. Sequence

The main feature of sequence is the ability to access the item in the index directly or to slice them.

```
#seq.py
x = ["monitor","keyboard","cpu","printer","mouse","paper",
"cables","laptops"]
print x[0]
print x[0:1]
print x[2:5]
print x[:4]
print x[4:]
print x[-4]
```

3.2.6. More on Strings

Everything in python is an object especially a string. String is of the class 'str(object)'.

Here are the most common features used:

- find(...)
- join(...)
- split(...)
- startswith(...)

basic string manupulation:

Pay ATTENTION to indentation!

```
#string.py
mystring = "Learning Practical Python"
if 'earning' in mystring:
    print 'found earning'
else:
    print 'did not find string pattern'
if mystring.startswith('Learn'):
    print 'found Learn startswith'
if mystring.find('earn') != -1:
    print 'found earn with find'
change = mystring.split()
```

```
print change
delimit = ';'
new = delimit.join(change)
print new
comm = new.split(';')
print comm
```

3.3. Modules

Python comes with a large library of modules that can be used for all sorts of tasks from database programming, web programming, to graphics and games. A module is a file that contains functions and variables defined for reuse. One of the first modules used was the string module that has a series of functions designed to manipulate strings. To use the module you import it as follows:

```
import string
```

Of course string is a standard library. You can build and save functions in another file and load them using import. Make sure the file you import has a 'py' extension. For example these two files:

```
#hellomodule.py
def hello():
    print "hello"
```

Create another file 'helloprog.py' and add the following:

```
#helloprog.py
import hellomodule
hellomodule.hello()
```

Then run **'python ./helloprog.py'**

It should print out 'hello' and it will also create a new file called 'hellomodule.pyc': The '.pyc' is a byte compiled file. It pre-compiles the file that is imported for speed on repeat usage. This is useful because importing libraries can take time to load depending on the library and the resources of the computer you are using.

3.3.1. sys Module

This is an important module that is used often when handling a list of arguments.

```
# arg1.py
import sys
print "script name", sys.argv[0]
#print "script arg", sys.argv[1]
#print "script arg list", sys.argv[1:]
```

First run the script as follows: ***'python ./arg1.py'***

Then uncomment out 'sys.argv[1]' and run ***'python ./arg1.py hello'***

Uncomment the last 'sys.argv[1:]' and run ***'python ./arg1.py 1 d hello'***

output:

```
script name arg1.py
script arg hello
script arg ['1', 'a', 'hello']
```

So now you get the idea that the first field in the list is the script name itself. A loop can easily cycle through the list.

```
# arg.py
import sys
for i in sys.argv:
   print i
```

Now run it: ***'python ./arg.py'***

Watch it loop through the arguments in the list. You can control your list using an 'if' statement.

```
# arg2.py
import sys
if len(sys.argv) > 1:
   print "Number of arguments:", len(sys.argv)-1
   for i in sys.argv[1:]:
      print i
else:
   print "no arguments..."
```

Run the following code above: ***python ./arg2.py arg1 arg2 hello***

As you see it's using a 'greater than 1' operator. There is always at least one item in the list which is the file itself. You need to separate the file name from the arguments. To do this, you will need to use -1.

3.3.2. Practical Usage:

Here is a practical example. **Pay ATTENTION to indentation!**

```
# square.py
import sys
def square(x):
    return x*x
x = int(sys.argv[1])
print 'square is %g' % square(x)
```

Run the program as follows: '***python ./square.py 4***' and it should return 16. However if you run it without an argument it will error. To fix you can easily add the 'if' statement below to the file above the function 'def square(x):'. No need to add the 'else' label as it is already implicit.

```
#square1.py
import sys
def square(x):
    return x*x
if len(sys.argv) !=2:
    print 'Need an integer'
    sys.exit(1)
x = int(sys.argv[1])
print 'square is %g' % square(x)
```

Run the following:"***python ./square1.py 4***" then run it again "***python ./square1.py***"

The 'if' evaluates that an argument exists or not. If not equal ('!=)' then exit. Remember that the first field in 'sys.argv[0]' is the file itself. Should you choose to use more than one integer or a string, the script will error out.

Using 'sys.argv' can be very useful when you find yourself using another program or script to talk to your python applications. You would be surprised how often this happens in the real world. The goal here is that you can create programs that require arguments and if the user doesn't enter an argument your code will catch it and print out a help statement that explains how to use the program.

3.3.3. from import

You can use both options 'from import' but note that it can make your code difficult to read. For example 'from sys import argv' and you could use 'argv' rather than 'sys.argv'. You can import all names in sys such as 'sys.exit, sys.path' in one shot like: **'import sys *'**. This could also make executables larger if compiled on windows. If you are following a coding style like "PEP 8", you will need to be specific and import only the modules you plan to use.

3.3.4. Testing a Module

Since all modules are objects, you can (and should) test them as you write. Make sure you use two underscores with no spaces between the underscores. For example: **Pay ATTENTION to indentation!**

```
# amodtest.py
if __name__ == '__main__':
    print 'access directly'
else:
    print 'from import'
```

Now run '***python ./amodtest.py***'.

```
output:
access directly
```

Run interactive prompt and confirm you are in same directory as 'amodtest.py'.

```
>>> import amodtest
from import
>>>
```

As you can see when the file is imported, the 'else' statement prints since it is not loaded directly. A more practical method would be:

```
# fmodtest.py
def square(x):
    return x*x
if __name__ == '__main__':
    print "testing square(4) directly", square(4)
```

If you run it directly, it should print out 16. Next, let's build another file and import it as follows:

```
# testmodf.py
import fmodtest
print "from import square(16)", fmodtest.square(16)
```

Notice this will only print the modules function 'def square(x)' from 'amodtest.py' and nothing after.

3.3.5. Summary

At this point you can build any algorithm you want. Having the ability to create your own functions gives you the power to create custom algorithms without importing additional libraries.

3.3.6. Exercises

1. Go through the examples above using the interactive interpreter.
2. Convert 'whileguess.py' into a function and call it 'guess()'.
3. Create a function to calculate Celsius and convert to Fahrenheit upon user input. Use a while loop to process the temperature until user enters 'x' to exit.

4. Using the following list (list="I will master strings"). Use a for loop to print the word 'master'.

4. Files

4.1. File

Working with files made simple.

4.1.1. The Basics

simple open example:

```
>>> blah=open("data.txt", 'w')
>>> blah.write("I am learning python\nI love python\nPython is great")
>>> blah.close()
>>>
```

4.1.2. Variations of Reading Data

File 'data.txt' contains the following:

```
I am learning python
I love python
Python is great
```

'file1.py' contains the following:

```
#!/usr/bin/python
# file1.py
blah = open("data.txt", "r")
print blah.readlines()
blah.close()
```

Results:

```
['I am learning python\n', 'I love python\n', 'python is great\n', '\n']
```

Let's make changes to 'file2.py' with the following:

```
#!/usr/bin/python
# file2.py
blah = open("data.txt", "r")
list = blah.readline()
for i in list:
    print i
blah.close()
```

results:

```
I
a
m
l
e
a
r
n
...
```

Here is something to remember: 'list = blah.read()' does the same except output is on separate lines. Try it out with the script above and review the differences.

```
#!/usr/bin/python
# file2.py
blah = open("data.txt", "r")
list = blah.readlines()
for i in list:
    print i
blah.close()
```

results:

```
I am learning python
I love python
python is great
```

Adjust 'file3.py' again:

```
#!/usr/bin/python
# file3.py
blah = open("data.txt", "r")
blah.seek(5)
print blah.readline()
blah.close()
```

results:

learning python

4.1.3. Parsing a file

In the previous chapters you learned to parse strings on a very limited bases. This section will provide a more detailed example on how to parse information in a very simple way. **Pay ATTENTION to indentation!**

```
#!/usr/bin/python
# parse.py
blah = open("data.txt", "r")
list=blah.readlines()
for i in list:
    if 'love' in i:
        new=i
print "print specific line 'love' in file"
print new
change=new.split()
print "print specific list in file as a list"
print change
print "print specific field in list 'love'"
print change[1]
for i in change:
    if 'python' in i:
        wow=i
print "search for specific field in list 'python' to print
wow"
blah.close()
```

Results:

```
print specific line 'love' in file
I love python
print specific list in file as a list
['I', 'love', 'python']
print specific field in list 'love'
love
search for specific field in list 'python' to print
python
```

The above example demonstrates the ability to only print a specific instance on a specific line of a file even if there might be more than one instance of the word 'python' in the file.

4.1.4. Binary Files

simple open binary file:

```
>>> blahbin = open ( 'binary.txt', 'wb' )
>>> blahbin.write ( 'write binary data.' )
>>> blahbin.close()
>>>
>>> blahbin = open ( 'binary.txt', 'rb' )
>>> print blahbin.read()
>>> blahbin.close()
>>>
```

4.1.5. Pickle

help('pickle')

Now that we can read and write string, what about lists, tuples, and dictionaries?

4.1.6. Let's Pickle

'Pickle' is used with databases and a few other python frameworks to assist with persistent data manipulation.

```
#!/usr/bin/python
#apickle.py
import pickle
filePickle = open ( 'pickleFile.txt', 'w' )
list = [ 'I', 'love', 'python', 1,2,3, 'ok' ]
list2 = { 'firstname': 'john', 'lastname': 'doe', 1: 'one'}
pickle.dump ( list, filePickle)
pickle.dump ( list2, filePickle)
filePickle.close()
```

Now look at the contents of the 'pickleFile.txt'. Open it up and take a look inside the file with your editor:

```
(lp0
S'I'
p1
aS'love'
p2
aS'python'
p3
aI1
aI2
aI3
aS'ok'
...
```

Create 'lpickle.py' and add the following: **Pay ATTENTION to indentation!**

```
#!/usr/bin/python
#lpickle.py
import pickle
filePickle = open ( 'pickleFile.txt' )
list = pickle.load ( filePickle)
list # used while in idle screen
for i in list:
    print i
dict = pickle.load (filePickle)
dict # used while in idle screen
for i in dict:
    print i
dict['firstname']
for i, j in dict.iteritems():
    print i, j
filePickle.close()
```

results:

```
I
love
python
1
2
3
ok
...
```

4.1.7. cPickle

A faster version of pickle is 'cPickle' which is a 'C' compiled version of pickle. This can be easily imported as follows:

```
import cPickle as pickle
```

Here is an example its essentially the same but while using idle you get a different effect using 'test1' or 'print test1':

```
>>>import cPickle as pickle
>>>
>>> test1 = ('I love python', 1, [1, 2, 3] )
>>> test1
('I love python', 1, [1, 2, 3])
>>>
>>> part1 = pickle.dumps(test1)
>>> part1
"(S'I love python'\nI1\n(lp1\nI1\naI2\naI3\natp2\n."
>>>
>>> print part1
(S'I love python'
I1
(lp1
I1
aI2
aI3
atp2
.
>>>
```

4.1.8. Python with Statement

Using the 'with' statement cuts down on exception handling for file stream by avoiding the need for 'try/finally' blocks of code. According to python documentation, the 'with' statement clarifies code previously by 'try...finally' blocks to ensure clean-up code is executed. Syntax is as follows:

```
with expression [as variable]: with-block
```

The expression is evaluated, and it should result in an object that supports the context management protocol '__enter__()' and '__exit__()' methods.

Let's write data to a file:

```
with open('output.txt', 'w') as f:
    f.write("Usual Hello World!")
```

The above 'with' statement will automatically close the file after nested block of code.

4.1.8.1. File Handling Modes

Table 4.1.: File Modes

Modes	Description
r	Opens file for reading only
rb	Opens file for reading binary only
r+	Opens file for both reading and writing
rb+	Opens binary file for reading and writing
w	Opens file for writing only
wb	Opens binary file for writing only
a	Opens a file for appending
ab	Opens a binary file for appending
a+	Opens a file for both appending and reading
ab+	Opens a file for both appending and reading in binary

4.1.8.2. File Attributes

Table 4.3.: File Attributes

Attribute	Description
file.closed	Returns true if closed
file.mode	Returns access mode of opened file
file.name	Returns the name of the file
file.softspace	Returns false if space explicitly required with print, otherwise true.

Example below:

```
#!/usr/bin/python
#filetest.py
f = open("dat.txt", "wb")
print "Name the file: ", f.name
print "Closed or open: ", f.closed
print "mode: ", f.mode
print "Softspace: ", f.softspace
```

Also note you did not need 'dat.txt' to run this script.

```
Results:
Name the file: dat.txt
Closed or open: False
mode: wb
Softspace: 0
```

4.1.9. Deep Binary Manipulation

Python has a limitation when working with binary files. The smallest unit you can work with is a byte. This can prove challenging when working with a data stream. Working with binary is beyond scope in this book and requires a firm foundation in computer software

But you can use bitwise operators to evaluate if a value is True or False. For example:

```
>>> x=3
>>> x&1!=0
True
>>> x&2!=0
True
>>> x&3!=0
True
>>> x&4!=0
False
```

4.1.9.1. bit string manipulation

This example converts string to binary using base2

```
>>>print int('001101',2)
13
>>>print int('0000011001',2)
25
>>>print "0x%x" % int('0011001',2)
0x25
```

Please note you didn't need to use 8 bits. My example above has 7 bits. However it took 1001 for the first value of 9 in the 1's place and the next 001 for 10's place making 19.

Conversion to Character requires an 8 bit maximum string.

```
>>> print chr(int('1111001',2))
y
>>> print chr(int('1111011',2))
{
```

Conversion of characters to integers.

```
>>> print int('1111011',2)
123
>>> ord('{')
123
```

Another way to convert individual bits.

```
>>> 1<<0
1
>>> 1<<1
2
>>> 1<<3
8
```

Conversion of Hex string to Integer

```
>>> int('0xff',16)
255
```

python 3 supports binary literal by adding b'01011' before the string to denote binary string.

The following is an example of bin(),oct(),and hex() conversion

```
>>> x=123
>>> bin(x)
'0b1111011'
```

Notice the literal 'b' encoded in the string representation. Literal data types are available in python3.0 or by importing future library

```
>>> oct(x)
'0173'
>>> hex(x)
'0x7b'
>>> format(x,'b')
'1111011'
>>> format(x,'o')
'173'
>>> format(x,'x')
'7b'
```

As you can see above 'int()' object handles a lot. ***help('int')***

```
class int(object)
| int(x=0) -> int or long
| int(x, base=10) -> int or long
|
| Convert a number or string to an integer, or return 0 if no arguments
| are given. If x is floating point, the conversion truncates towards zero.
| If x is outside the integer range, the function returns a long instead.
|
| If x is not a number or if base is given, then x must be a string or
| Unicode object representing an integer literal in the given base. The
| literal can be preceded by '+' or '-' and be surrounded by whitespace.
| The base defaults to 10. Valid bases are 0 and 2-36. Base 0 means to
| interpret the base from the string as an integer literal.
| >>> int('0b100', base=0)
| 4
```

4.1.10. Binary Struct

The structure of 'struct' to pack and unpack. pack() and unpack() require a string to define how binary data is structured.

```
#mystruct.py
import struct
# i represents integer
# c represents character
bdata=struct.pack("icc", 42,b'A', b'Z')
print(bdata)
# unpack yields a tuple of data
tdata=struct.unpack("icc",bdata)
print(tdata)
```

Results:

*AZ

(42, 'A', 'Z')

The struct module performs conversions between Python values and 'C' struct's represented as a Python string. Pack and Unpack require character formats to determine structure:

Format	Type
x	no values
c	char
b	signed int
B	unsigned int
?	bool
h	int short
H	unsigned short
i	int
I	unsigned int
l	long
L	unsigned long
q	long long
Q	unsigned long long
f	float

d	double
s	char[]
p	char[]
P	void *

Below is an example of reading parsing a jpeg file and extracting size

```
#readjpg.py
import sys
import binascii
import struct
signature=[
  binascii.unhexlify(b'FFD8FFD8'),
  binascii.unhexlify(b'FFD8FFE0'),
  binascii.unhexlify(b'FFD8FFE1') ]
with open(sys.argv[1],'rb') as file:
  first_four_bytes=file.read(4)
  if first_four_bytes in signature:
    print("JPEG found.")
  else: print("This is not a JPEG file.")
  print first_four_bytes
  print binascii.hexlify(first_four_bytes)
  second=file.read(1)
  while (ord(second) !=0xDA):
    while (ord(second) !=0xFF): second=file.read(1)
    while (ord(second) ==0xFF): second=file.read(1)
    if (ord(second) >=0xC0 and ord(second) <=0xC3):
      print binascii.hexlify(file.read(3))
      print struct.unpack('>HH',file.read(4))
```

4.1.11. Summary

At this point, you have the ability to program just about anything using a structured top down method. Python works best as a higher level programming language and is not a practical language to work at a low level with large binary data. The binary example in this section will only be used as a reference and will not be discussed or used later in this book due to the complexity.

4.1.12. Exercises

- Write two files. A library function to open and parse your file searching for the quantity of python in the sample file below. Create another file to import that library and print out lines (3-6), and replace every instance of keyword 'python'.

Sample file:

```
I love python
I will master python
python is the greatest
python pays big money
python will set you free
I will make a python script
python will be my future
All my programs will be replaced with python
only python
python python
```

5. Exceptions

5.1. Exceptions

There is no doubt whatsoever that you have already watched your programs crash. Every time the crash occurs it prints out the all too familiar message "Traceback (most recent call last):" followed by your File 'name.py' a line number and some additional information telling you why the program crashed. The bottom line is that checking for errors is tedious and boring. However, you must master the basics of this section before moving forward in your software development career. Please note that exceptions are not the absolute answer to preventing your programs from crashing. Code can be very complex and some problems just can't be predicted. Lets see an example and crash a program:

```
#!/usr/bin/python
#tro.py
x=int(raw_input("Enter a number: "))
print x
```

Run the program using any letter such as 'a' and you will get the following results:

Pay ATTENTION to indentation!

```
Enter a number: a
Traceback (most recent call last):
  File "./tro.py", line 3, in <module>
    x=int(raw_input("Enter a number: "))
ValueError: invalid literal for int() with base 10: 'a'
```

The error is a ValueError. The 'raw_input' is wrapped with 'int()'. This line expected an integer and you substituted an integer with a letter. To guide the user to enter the correct type of data, we rewrite 'tro.py' with the following information.

```
#!/usr/bin/python
#tro1.py
try:
    x=int(raw_input("Enter a number: "))
    print x
except ValueError:
    print "You did not enter a number"
```

Another way to write it:

```
#!/usr/bin/python
#tro2.py
try:
    x=int(raw_input("Enter a number: "))
    print x
except:
    print "You did not enter a number"
```

This would be considered a catch all for multiple exceptions. However, this is not good programming practice. It's recommended that you understand the different types of exceptions that could occur. It's very easy to have multiple exceptions for a routine block of code. For example:

```
#!/usr/bin/python
#try3.py
try:
    x=int(raw_input("Enter a number: "))
    print x
except EOFError: print "why did you exit early"
except ValueError:
    print "You did not enter a number"
```

Run this program (Do not enter a number or letter) then type 'Ctrl-d' to exit the program. . When you exit early, you hit the EOF error or 'End Of File'. .

5.1.1. Raise Exception

There are cases in which you want to your program to operate as intended and still raise an exception when needed. You can create your own exceptions and raise them yourself. The following demonstrates how to raise your own exceptions. Don't forget to 'import sys' package.

```
#!/usr/bin/python
#raise.py
import sys
def letserror():
    raise RuntimeError('Force the error')
def main():
    letserror()
main()
```

Results (the line numbers could be a little different):

Pay ATTENTION to indentation!

```
Traceback (most recent call last):
    File "raise.py", line 7, in <module>
        main()
    File "raise.py", line 6, in main
        letserror()
    File "raise.py", line 4, in letserror
        raise RuntimeError('Force the error')
RuntimeError: Force the error
```

However this does not look so clean. Below is a slight modification:

Pay ATTENTION to indentation!

```
#!/usr/bin/python
#raise2.py
import sys
def letserror():
    raise RuntimeError('Force the error')
def main(num):
    try:
        letserror()
```

```
        except Exception, err:
            sys.stderr.write(str(err))
    main(0)
```

You do have quite a bit control in how you print your error messages out. For example you could replace 'sys.stderr.write' with the following: "sys.stderr.write("%s\n" % str(err))". The object 'sys.stderr' is part of the Unix standard input, output and error pipe. Let's put this into action. Here is a more practical example:

Pay ATTENTION to indentation!

```
#!/usr/bin/python
#raise3.py
import sys
def letserror():
    raise RuntimeError('Force the error')
def main(num):
    try:
        if num < 3:
            letserror()
        else:
            blah=num*num
            print "my number is", blah
    except Exception, err:
        sys.stderr.write("%s your number %s is less than
3\n" % (str(err),num))
main(2)
```

If you change 'main(2)' to '3' it will square your number, however if it's less than '3' or (< 3), the error will raise and you can give the user a detailed explanation.

5.1.2. Finally

The finally stanza is guaranteed to run even if the try block raises an exception. This makes it ideal for cleanup or 'close()'. For example:

Pay ATTENTION to indentation!

```
#!/usr/bin/python
#raise4.py
import sys
def letserror():
    raise RuntimeError('Force the error')
def main(num):
    try:
        if num < 3:
            letserror()
        else:
            blah=num*num
            print "my number is", blah
    except Exception, err:
        sys.stderr.write("%s your num %s less than 3\n"
% (str(err),num))
    finally:
        print "okay I could close the file or end this etc..."
main(2)
```

You will notice that the finally stanza runs if an error is raised or not.

5.1.3. Best Practice

Plenty of examples have been listed above. At the very least, the base exception class 'Exception(Base Exception)' should be utilized as a default solution for handling multiple cases. Try it with a letter, number, or no data, and 'ctrl-z'.

```
try:
    x=int(raw_input("Enter a number: "))
exception Exception, e:
    print e
```

5.1.4. Ignore Exception

Add 'pass' which is a null operation.

```
try:
    x=int(raw_input("Enter a number: "))
exception Exception, e:
    pass
```

5.1.5. Summary

Make every effort to master exception handling because it will save you when troubleshooting code and more than likely improve the quality of your software development. No exercises are required in this section because you should continue the practice of implementing exception handling moving forward.

6. OOP

6.1. Object Oriented Programming

6.1.1. Intro

So far you have been creating programs in a procedural way using functions and blocks of statements. With a slight twist you can wrap your functions into an object, and advance to understanding the concept of the object oriented programming paradigm. Without realizing it, you have already been using certain aspects of object oriented programming but in a procedural way.

6.1.2. Objects

By now, you are familiar with features such as strings, integers, dictionaries, and functions. These are all objects. The string object has methods which provide additional ways to manipulate the string. Using the 'dot syntax' you can access the objects attributes such as "string A.lower()". So from the beginning we have been accessing the methods of each of our objects. You can also create new instance of the object known as instantiation. In essence they are 'datatypes' and can be tested with a built in function 'type'.

```
>>> dat='a string'
>>> print type('dat')
<type 'str'>
```

The 'dot syntax' would apply easily. Checking your 'type', you find it to be a class string object or 'str(object)'. Here is an example of a class object easily tested using 'type'. Don't forget you will still need to indent your text after the class statement. Reminder: There are no spaces between the underscore symbols. **Finally as always, pay ATTENTION to indentation!**

```
>>> class orphan():
...     def __init__(self):
...         self.arg1=arg1
...
>>> print type(orphan)
<type 'classobj'>
>>>
```

Objects store data by using variables that belong to the object. The variables belong to the object or class as fields. Functions work the same, they are called methods of a class. So basically fields and methods are attributes of a class.

6.1.3. Self and Class

A class is created by using the keyword 'class' like "class orphan():". What makes this different from a function or (method) is the name specifier of 'self'. The value of 'self' is the name itself which refers to the object itself. Think of 'self' like a pointer in C++. If you have a class called 'blahClass' and an instance of the class called 'blahObj'. You call the method of the object like 'blahObj.method(arg1)', python will convert it as "BlahClass.method(blahObj,arg1)". Even if you have a method with no arguments, you still have to define a method with the self argument. Here is a practical example:

```
#classhello.py
class hello:
   def blah(self):
      print "Hello world, again"
```

```
a=hello() # pointer location in memory
a.blah() # print method of class
hello().blah() # another way to access the class
```

As you can see self exists and it takes no parameters.

Results:

```
Hello world, again
Hello world, again
```

6.1.4. __init__

The '__init__' method initializes as soon as the object is instantiated. We don't call the method '__init__' (our constructor). We merely pass it arguments. For example:

Pay ATTENTION to indentation!

```
#classinit.py
class hello:
    def __init__(self,name):
        self.name=name
    def blah(self):
        print "Hello world, my name is",self.name
a=hello('William')
a.blah()
```

Results:

```
Hello world, my name is William
```

Now pass more arguments:

```
#name.py
class hello:
    def __init__(self,l,f):
        self.last=l
        self.first=f
    def blah(self):
        print "My first name is", self.first
        print "My last name is", self.last
a=hello('Doe', 'John')
a.blah()
```

Results:

```
My first name is John
My last name is Doe
```

Here is another example:

```
#shop.py
class cart():
    def __init__(self):
        self.food = "beans"
        self.amt = 0
    def buyfood(self,amt):
        self.amt += amt
        print "You purchased" ,amt,"cans",self.food
checkout = cart()
checkout.buyfood(5)
```

Results:

```
You purchased 5 cans beans
```

6.1.5. Destructor

Here is a small example of a destructor. Though I hardly ever use destructors in my code, they do exist and can be useful.

```
#des.py
class Des():
    def __init__(self, x):
        self.x = x
        print self.x, 'ready'
    def __del__(self):
        print self.x-1, 'destroyed'
x = Des(1)
```

Results:

```
1 ready
0 destroyed
```

6.1.6. Inheritance

You can develop a class that inherits the values of another class. This example shows you how to inherit the 'first()' class in the 'second()' class as 'class second(first)':

Pay ATTENTION to indentation!

```
#in.py
class first():
    n = 0
    def __init__(self, color='red'):
        self.color = color
    def Hello1(self):
        print "Hello from first class!"
    def Color(self):
        print "My color from first class", self.color
class second(first):
    def Hello2(self):
        print "Hello from second class!"
        print self.n, "is my favorite number"
a0=first()
a0.Color()
print '——-'
a1=first('blue')
a1.Hello1()
a1.Color()
print '——-'
a2=second('white')
a2.Hello1()
a2.Hello2()
a2.Color()
```

6.1.7. __private

The Double underscore prefix is dealt with using name mangling to effectively make it private within class or object.

6.1.8. The Kung Fu of Class

All classes in python are derived from a special top down parent class called object that may or may not be explicitly derived.

```
class KungFu(Object):
```

In Python a class that is derived from the 'superclass' is called the 'subclass'. Let's inherent from the parent class in the example below.

```
#kungfu.py
class KungFu(object):
    mystr="the master"
    pass
class Master(KungFu):
    pass
teacher=Master.mystr
print teacher
```

Results:

```
The master
```

Now override attribute value in subclass.

```
#kungfu1.py
class KungFu(object):
    mystr="the master"
class Master(KungFu):
    mystr="Student is not the master"
teacher=Master.mystr
print teacher
```

Results:

```
Student is not the master
```

Execute method from parent class inside subclass.

```
#kungfu2.py
class KungFu(object):
    mystr="the master"
    def crane(self):
        print "crane kick"
class Master(KungFu):
```

```
    mystr="Student is not the master"
teacher=Master()
teacher.crane()
```

Results:

```
crane kick
```

Override parent class with sublcass.

```
#kungfu3.py
class KungFu(object):
    mystr="the master"

    def crane(self):

        print "crane kick"
class Master(KungFu):
    mystr="Student is not the master"

    def crane(self,bstr):

        print "must learn crane kick"
teacher=Master()
teacher.crane(1)
```

Results:

```
must learn crane kick
```

6.1.9. Iterate Over Unknown Objects

Time and again I have found myself working with large applications that are poorly documented. Below is a handy method to parse potentially unknown objects via subclass. Pretend 'class bar' has a lot of methods (perhaps thousands of methods) and you want to generate a list for easy lookup. This is a great troubleshooting exercise to get a summary of methods contained within a class.

Pay ATTENTION to indentation!

```
#!/usr/bin/python
#unknown.py
class bar:
    def blah(self):

        print "cool"
```

```
        def strange(self):
            print "wow"
        def nice(self):
            print "very cool now"
        def bazinga(self):
            print "bazinga"
    class foo(bar):
        def __iter__(self): # iterate unknown
            return iter(vars(bar)) # vars built-in attr
    a=foo()
    for i in a:
        print i
```

Results:

```
__module__
bazinga
blah
strange
__doc__
nice
```

As you venture further into OOP. Subclassing a parent class to change an attribute will occur frequently and eventually you will want to track your own methods or an existing method this is a brief example on how to look at your work from a different perspective.

6.1.10. Multiple Inheritence

I'm not crazy about using multiple inheritance or super. Multiple inheritance should be avoid and replaced with design patterns and if you plan to use 'super()' it's usage should be consistent. In class hierarchy, super should be used everywhere or nowhere. Mixing super and classic call is extremely confusing and doesn't make things explicit. Instead focus on customizing classes and leverage methods such as '__getattr__', '__setattr__' and '__getattribute__'.

Please do not type the following code below, it is only an example: Use the IDLE interpreter and type help(super)

```
>>>help(super)
    class super(object)
    | super(type, obj) -> bound super object; requires isin-
stance(obj, type)
    | super(type) -> unbound super object
    | super(type, type2) -> bound super object; requires is-
subclass(type2, type)
    | Typical use to call a cooperative superclass method:
    | class C(B):
    | def meth(self, arg):
    etc...
```

6.1.11. Summary

These are the basic terminologies of object-oriented programming and mastering these concepts will allow you to build and scale large applications.

Part II.

Intermediate

Part II

-Improving your code

7. Cool Features of Python

7.1. Cool Features of Python

7.1.1. List Comprehension

A list comprehension is a feature that allows you to create lists without resorting to using a built-in function or filter for every iterable item. The following is an example of populating a list using basic iteration and a filter or flow statement.

```
#list.py
output=[]
for i in range(10):
    if i > 5:
        output.append(i)
print output
```

The following is an example using a comprehensive list:

```
#list2.py
output=[i for i in range(10) if i> 3]
print output
```

Removing the indentation and encapsulating your statements allows you to evaluate expressions within the list. Let's take a look at a few more examples.

```
#list3.py
square=[i**2 for i in range(10)]
factor=[2**i for i in range(10)]
evenSquare=[x for x in square if x % 2 == 0]
oddSquare=[x for x in square if x % 2 == 1]
print square
print factor
print evenSquare
print oddSquare
```

Results:

```
[0, 1, 4, 9, 16, 25, 36, 49, 64, 81]
[1, 2, 4, 8, 16, 32, 64, 128, 256, 512]
[0, 4, 16, 36, 64]
[1, 9, 25, 49, 81]
```

7.1.2. Lambda

Lambda is a special function or anonymous function created at runtime. To illustrate the differences, see below.

This is a regular function:

```
#nlam.py
def blah(x): return x*x
print blah(2)
```

This is a lambda function

```
#lam.py
blah= lambda x: x*x
print blah(2)
```

They do exactly the same thing, but the lambda expression is does not contain the return stanza. You can put a lambda definition anywhere a function exists, and you don't need to assign it to a variable. Lambda functions are a matter of style. They are not required and can be easily substituted using a function. If you find yourself creating lots of short functions, then lambdas could be a useful solution. Here is a more practical example:

```
#lambda.py
foo=[1,2,3,4,5,6]
print filter(lambda x: x % 2 == 0, foo)
print filter(lambda x: x % 2 == 0, (x for x in range(1,7)))
blah=[x for x in range(1,7) if x %2 == 0]
print blah
```

Results:

```
[2, 4, 6]
[2, 4, 6]
[2, 4, 6]
```

Notice that the last expression is replaced with list comprehension.

7.1.3. Assert

Assert is commonly used in debugging code. The format for assert is (assert <test>, <message>). For example..

```
#assert.py
blah=int(raw_input("enter number greater than 3: "))
assert blah !=3, 'strange why did you enter 3'
```

Results:

```
enter number greater than 3: 3
Traceback (most recent call last):
  File "assert.py", line 9, in <module>
    assert blah !=3, 'strange why did you enter 3'
AssertionError: strange why did you enter 3
```

The statement asserts that something is true. If you enter '3', an error would be raised and the assert message will be passed at standard output. If you have a list such as:

```
list=['hello']
assert len(list) >= 1
```

The assertion is true and no message is passed. You might need an assertion to enforce that something is in a list, because you may have designed your program to operate with at least one item in the list. If that list is empty, you want your program to exit out with an assert message that stipulates why the program exited.

7.1.4. eval

'Eval' is another example of a function that evaluates a string. The program below will also demonstrate the lack of trust from which you receive the string from your source.

```
#aeval.py
a='a'
blah=raw_input("enter numbers: ")
print blah
print "my eval is: ", eval(blah)
print "my type is: ", type(blah)
```

Test this program '8' different times with the following sources "(3, 2.5, a, b, 'b', 2*3, '2*3', "len('hello')")"

7.1.5. exec

This is executed dynamically at run time. Depending on your objective, it can be very useful to mix python with bash or another scripting language.

```
>>>exec 'print "hello"'
```

Here is a more practical example:

```
#exec.py
code = """
def foo(x): return x+1
print 'hello world.'
"""
exec code
print foo(3)
```

Results:

```
hello world.
4
```

7.1.6. repr

'Repr' simply displays a printable representation of the object. For example:

```
#rep.py
i=[]
i.append('blah')
print repr(i)
```

This is useful if you are in the middle of coding and simply forgot what a variable might be and need to return a printable representation of the object. You can control the level if '__repr__' is defined.

7.1.7. switch or case

Python does not have a switch statement also known as a case statement like many of the other programming languages. Blogs from a search engine will reveal as much. It was not designed for that need. The elegance of a properly used if/else statement provides additional tests as well as equality checks and a default response. Using a dictionary doesn't have those features and you might find yourself throwing an exception more than once. This is a choice that can lead to creative code inspiring you to strive for improvements. A typical 'C' statement below would be as follows: Do not type out example code below.

```
switch(num){
        case val1: /* code for val1 */
            break;
        case val2: /* code for val2 */
            break;
        default: /* default code nothing chosen */
            break;
}
```

Here is a practical example in bash that you can test if you do not have 'C' installed or knowledge of 'C'.

```
function case1(){
echo "print case1 statement"
}
function case2(){
echo "print case2 statement"
}
function case3(){
echo "print case3 statement"
}
function case4(){
echo "print case4 statement"
}
echo "1) case1"
echo "2) case2"
echo "3) case3"
echo "3) case4"
echo -e "enter number 1-4: "
read blah
case $blah in
1) case1
;;
2) case2
;;
3) case3
;;
4) case4
esac
```

Here is an example of a case or switch statement created using a dictionary:

```
#case.py
print "0: exit"
print "1: sqr 4"
print "2: list 1-10"
print "3: print even list 1-10"
data=int(raw_input("Enter 0-3: "))
x=4
def exit():
    print "you exited"
def sqr():
```

```
    print x*x
def list():
    for x in range(10):
        print x
def even():
    for x in range(1,10):
        if x % 2 == 0:
            print x
blah={0: exit, 1: sqr, 2: list, 3: even }
blah[data]()
```

This can be re-written using lambda but you run into an additional limitation such as the inability to print statements. It is not recommended to pass arguments to a lambda function while choosing an item in the dictionary to run at the same time. It defeats the purpose of the switch. The idea is to write code that can be easily understood. Lambda must be an expression not a statement. The if-else is still the best option.

7.2. Converting to OOP with pass

Converting your procedural programs to the object oriented programming style can be a fun exercise. Most of the time you simply begin with an idea and want to start writing code immediately. Keep in mind that this approach falls far below the standard for enterprise application design which would begin using 'OOP' prototyping of new classifications from the start. It is possible that your idea could blossom into something that requires an enterprise level programming paradigm. The examples below retain comments in the code through conversion. For example, let's say you have an apartment complex with the following:

10 units with 2 bedrooms
8 covered parking slots
1 pool

x rooms
15 people

Calculations:

rooms=10*2
capacity of filled rooms
uncovered parking

The idea is to start creating the variables first, then begin creating the calculations.

```
unit=10
parking=8
pool=1
rooms=20
people=15

capacity=people/rooms
uncovered=100-(parking/people*100)
rooms=10*2
freerooms=rooms-people
```

Now that we have all of our variables in place, we need to print them out.

```
print "The complex is at %g" % capacity.
print "There are %g percent people with uncovered park-
ing" % uncovered
print "We have %g rooms" % rooms
print "We have %g free rooms left" % freerooms
```

Create script below:

```
#apartment.py
# required information:10 units with 2 bedrooms,
#8 covered parking
#1 pool, x rooms, 15 people
unit=10
parking=8
pool=1
rooms=20
people=15
capacity=float(people)/rooms
uncovered=100-(float(parking)/people*100)
rooms=10*2
freerooms=rooms-people
print "The complex is at %g" % capacity
```

```
print "There are %g percent people with uncovered parking" % uncovered
print "We have %g rooms" % rooms
print "We have %g free rooms left" % freerooms
```

7.2.1. Convert to OOP using pass

Create the class called complex. Next, call the method object with 'myCo', and rename initial variables with 'myCo.var' etc... Notice which variables are not called.

```
#apartment1.py
# required information:10 units with 2 bedrooms,
#8 covered parking
#1 pool, x rooms, 15 people
class complex:
    pass
myCo=complex()
myCo.unit=10
myCo.parking=8
myCo.pool=1
myCo.rooms=20
myCo.people=15
capacity=float(myCo.people)/myCo.rooms
uncovered=100-(float(myCo.parking)/myCo.people*100)
myCo.rooms=10*2
freerooms=myCo.rooms-myCo.people
print "The complex is at %g capacity" % capacity
print "There are %g percent people with uncovered parking" % uncovered
print "We have %g rooms" % myCo.rooms
print "We have %g free rooms left" % freerooms
```

7.2.2. Initialize method of conversion

Create the method '__init__' and add the arguments. Next copy and paste the original variables in to the '__init__' method block, then remove 'MyCo' and add self. to each variable. Remove the unit value, add the argument name and lastly comment out the original variables.

```
#apartment2.py
# required information:10 units with 2 bedrooms,
#8 covered parking
#1 pool, x rooms, 15 people
class complex:
    def __init__(self, unit, parking, pool, rooms, people):
        self.unit=unit
        self.parking=parking
        self.pool=pool
        self.rooms=rooms
        self.people=people

myCo=complex(10,8,1,20,15)
#myCo.unit=10
#myCo.parking=8
#myCo.pool=1
#myCo.rooms=20
#myCo.people=15
#comment out the next two blocks
capacity=float(myCo.people)/myCo.rooms
uncovered=100-(float(myCo.parking)/myCo.people*100)
myCo.rooms=10*2
freerooms=myCo.rooms-myCo.people
print "The complex is at %g capacity" % capacity
print "There are %g percent people with uncovered parking" % uncovered
print "We have %g rooms" % myCo.rooms
print "We have %g free rooms left" % freerooms
```

7.2.3. Last part conversion

Please note that you are commenting out large blocks of code to be converted over as you work. Next, create a method to calculate your values and a method to print out your values. Then rename each variable to 'self.name' notation and initialize 'calc' method and the 'print' method.

```
#apartment3.py
# required information:10 units with 2 bedrooms,
#8 covered parking
#1 pool, x rooms, 15 people
```

```
class complex:
    def __init__(self, unit, parking, pool, rooms, peo-
ple):
        self.unit=unit
        self.parking=parking
        self.pool=pool
        self.rooms=rooms
        self.people=people
    def calc(self):
        self.capacity=float(self.people)/self.rooms
        self.uncovered=100-(float(self.parking)/self.people*100)
        self.rooms=10*2
        self.freerooms=self.rooms-self.people
    def result(self):
        print "The complex is at %g capacity" % self.capacity
        print "There are %g percent people with uncovered
parking" % self.uncovered
        print "We have %g rooms" % self.rooms
        print "We have %g free rooms left" % self.freerooms
myCo=complex(10,8,1,20,15)
myCo.calc() # these are tied together initialize
myCo.result() # these are tied together
#myCo.unit=10
#myCo.parking=8
#myCo.pool=1
#myCo.rooms=20
#myCo.people=15
#comment out the next two blocks
#capacity=float(myCo.people)/myCo.rooms
#uncovered=100-(float(myCo.parking)/myCo.people*100)
#myCo.rooms=10*2
#freerooms=myCo.rooms-myCo.people
#print "The complex is at %g capacity" % capacity
#print "There are %g percent people with uncovered park-
ing" % uncovered
#print "We have %g rooms" % myCo.rooms
#print "We have %g free rooms left" % freerooms
```

7.2.4. Test Locally

Once this is complete, you have the option to make it more flexible by adding an if statement to the the end of your program. This allows your code to be imported for external use.

```
if __name__=="__main__":
    myCo=complex(10,8,1,20,15)
    myCo.calc()
    myCo.result()
```

You can now import this into other scripts and/or make minor tweaks and customizations to existing code.

7.3. Generators

A generator is a function that can stop at any arbitrary point in its body and return a value to the caller, then resume from where it left off. As an example here is a simple function:

```
# gen1.py
def mygen():
    print "generate"
    yield 1
    print "my"
    yield 2
    print "list"
if __name__=="__main__":
    print mygen()
```

When executed we get the following: "<generator object mygen at 0xb788e694>"

The hex dump generator above will have a different register number.

We get a different result if we apply a loop as follows:

```
#gtest1a.py
from gen1 import *
blah=mygen()
for i in blah:
    print i
```

outputs:

```
generate
1
my
2
list
```

Note that the 'yield' statement is a keyword function in past versions and you needed a generator facility to import. Now, you can call the yield directly at the IDLE interpeter:

```
>>> from gen1 import *
>>> blah=mygen()
>>> blah.next()
generate
1
>>> blah.next()
my
2
>>> blah.next()
list
Traceback (most recent call last):
File "<stdin>", line 1, in <module>
StopIteration
>>>
```

The goal with the generators is to minimize loading data into large lists consuming enormous amounts of memory. Generators are often used with algorithms such as Fibonacci and factorial sequences. This also requires enormous memory and processing speed. Below is a script that shows various uses of the yield keyword. Notice the output when the yield or print statement is printed. Also notice the use of list comprehensions.

```
#mlist.py
def mlist():
    print "a"
```

```
    yield "one"
    print "b"
    yield "two"
    print "c"
    yield "three"
    print "d"
    yield "four"
    print "e"
    yield "five"
    print "f"
    yield "six"
    print "g"
    yield "seven"
    print "h"
for i in mlist():
    print i
for x,y in zip([0], mlist()):
    print x, y
for x,y in zip([0,1,2], mlist()):
    print x, y
for x,y in zip([j for j in range(9) if j>5], mlist()):
    print x,y
for x,y in zip([j for j in range(9)], mlist()):
    print x,y
for x,y in zip([j for j in range(9)], mlist()):
    print x
for x,y in zip([j for j in range(9)], mlist()):
    print y
import itertools
list(itertools.islice(mlist(),4))
print "blah"
list(itertools.islice(mlist(),10))
```

Here is another example of a generator using a file.

```
#blah.txt
Hello world
This is you
how are you
wow more data
this is cool
```

```
I can not wait to
jump in
the air
```

Generator script tfile1:

```
#tfile1.py
f=open("blah.txt","r")
def mygen(f):
    for i in r.readlines():
        yield i
if __name__=="__main__":
    a=mygen(f)
    for i in a:
        print i
    f.close()
```

tfile2 script:

```
#tfile2.py
from tfile1 import *
mygen(f)
for x,y in zip([z for z in range(9)], mygen(f)):
    print repr(x),repr(y)
for x,y in zip([z for z in range(9) if z > 5], mygen(f)):
    print x
print "____________________"
for x,y in zip([z for z in range(9) if z > 5], mygen(f)):
    print y
print "____________________"
for i in mygen(f):
    print i
print list(mygen(f))
f.close()
```

Results:

```
0 'Hello world\n'
1 'This is you \n'
2 'how are you \n'
3 'wow more data\n'
4 'this is cool\n'
5 'I can not wait to \n'
6 'jump in \n'
7 'the air\n'
```

Notice what can and cannot be done. Note also that each entry is a yield statement.

7.4. Threads

Python has the ability to perform multiple tasks at the same time. As you progress with python programming, you may need to use multiple threads to complete your job. Examples may include parsing through multiple files, copying files to multiple servers, or performing miscellaneous tasks for multiple miscellaneous jobs. However according to 'Guid Von Rossum', creator of python scripting language.

“"Unfortunately, for most mortals, thread programming is just too hard to get right...Even in Python – every time someone gets into serious thread programming, they send me tons of bug reports, and half of them are subtle bugs in the Python interpreter, have of them are subtle problems in their own understanding of the consequences of multiple threads..."

On that note, I plan to introduce threads in the simplest way. We will utilize the 'ping' tool on Linux or Windows. Here is the "ping -h" on Linux:

Usage: ping [-LRUbdfnqrvVaAD] [-c count] [-i interval] [-w deadline]
[-p pattern] [-s packetsize] [-t ttl] [-I interface]
[-M pmtudisc-hint] [-m mark] [-S sndbuf]
[-T tstamp-options] [-Q tos] [hop1 ...] destination

Next will use “ping -c 1 ipaddress”. Before you begin, you will need an IP address that you can ping and one that you can't. On Linux you can run 'ifconfig' (ipconfig for windows)to find out what addresses are currently assigned.

```
ifconfig
lan0 Link encap:Ethernet HWaddr 00:1c:bf:c9:6c:9a
inet addr:10.59.26.111 Bcast:10.59.31.255 Mask:255.255.224.0
inet6 addr: fe80::21c:bfff:fec9:6c9a/64 Scope:Link
UP BROADCAST RUNNING MULTICAST MTU:1500 Metric:1
RX packets:6488 errors:0 dropped:0 overruns:0 frame:0
TX packets:5226 errors:0 dropped:0 overruns:0 carrier:0
collisions:0 txqueuelen:1000
RX bytes:4642005 (4.4 MiB) TX bytes:1031603 (1007.4 KiB)
```

Let's say 10.59.26.111 is a ping-able address. When I ping 10.59.26.111 I get the following:

```
PING 10.59.26.111 (10.59.26.111) 56(84) bytes of data.
64 bytes from 10.59.26.111: icmp_req=1 ttl=64 time=0.045 ms
64 bytes from 10.59.26.111: icmp_req=2 ttl=64 time=0.039 ms
^C
— 10.59.26.111 ping statistics —
2 packets transmitted, 2 received, 0% packet loss, time 999ms
rtt min/avg/max/mdev = 0.039/0.042/0.045/0.003 ms
```

It will keep pinging the address until I input 'Ctrl-C' to break out of it. Now, let's look at what happens when we ping a non-ping-able address like 10.59.26.112.

```
PING 10.59.26.112 (10.59.26.112) 56(84) bytes of data.
From 10.59.26.111 icmp_seq=2 Destination Host Unreachable
From 10.59.26.111 icmp_seq=3 Destination Host Unreachable
From 10.59.26.111 icmp_seq=4 Destination Host Unreachable
From 10.59.26.111 icmp_seq=6 Destination Host Unreachable
From 10.59.26.111 icmp_seq=7 Destination Host Unreachable
From 10.59.26.111 icmp_seq=8 Destination Host Unreachable
^C
— 10.59.26.112 ping statistics —
8 packets transmitted, 0 received, +6 errors, 100% packet loss, time 7017ms
pipe 3
```

The most important thing you need to understand this section is one address you know you can ping successfully like google or yahoo and one address you know will not ping. You might use your Loopback device (127.0.0.1) and local Ethernet device for this experiment.

Let's create a script to test this:

```
#!/usr/bin/python
#ping.py
import os
num1=2 # can't ping
num2=1 # can ping
dat="ping -c 1 127.0.0.%d" % num1
dat1="ping -c 1 127.0.0.%d" % num2
a=os.system(dat1)
a=os.system(dat)
```

When you run the script you should get the following: *"python ping.py"*

```
PING 127.0.0.2 (127.0.0.2) 56(84) bytes of data.
From 127.0.0.1 icmp_seq=1 Destination Host Unreachable
— 127.0.0.2 ping statistics —
1 packets transmitted, 0 received, +1 errors, 100% packet loss, time 0ms
PING 127.0.0.1 (127.0.0.1) 56(84) bytes of data.
64 bytes from 127.0.0.1: icmp_req=1 ttl=64 time=0.038 ms
— 127.0.0.1 ping statistics —
1 packets transmitted, 1 received, 0% packet loss, time 0ms
rtt min/avg/max/mdev = 0.038/0.038/0.038/0.000 ms
```

* Notice: I started with the address that is unreachable first. Next, we create a function for this.

```
#ping1.py
import os
num1=2
num2=1
dat="ping -c 1 127.0.0.%d" % num1
dat1="ping -c 1 127.0.0.%d" % num2
#a=os.system(dat1)
#a=os.system(dat)
def mythread(x):
    a=os.system(x)
mythread(dat1)
mythread(dat)
```

When we run it we get the same results. Now, we will utilize python module threads.

```
>>> help('threading')
Help on module threading:
NAME
threading - Thread module emulating a subset of Java's thread-
ing model.
FILE
/usr/lib/python2.6/threading.py
MODULE DOCS
http://docs.python.org/library/threading
CLASSES
__builtin__.object
thread._local
_Verbose(__builtin__.object)
Thread
class Thread(_Verbose)
...
```

Ping test:

```
#python ping2.py
from threading import Thread
import os
num1=2
num2=1
dat="ping -c 1 127.0.0.%d" % num1
dat1="ping -c 1 127.0.0.%d" % num2
def mythread(x):
    a=os.system(x)
a=Thread(target=mythread, args=(dat1,))
c=Thread(target=mythread, args=(dat,))
b=Thread(target=mythread, args=(dat,))
a.start()
b.start()
c.start()
```

Here are the results:

```
PING 127.0.02 (127.0.0.2) 56(84) bytes of data.
PING 127.0.01 (127.0.01) 56(84) bytes of data.
64 bytes from 127.0.01: icmp_req=1 ttl=64 time=0.022
ms
— 127.0.01 ping statistics —
1 packets transmitted, 1 received, 0% packet loss, time
0ms
rtt min/avg/max/mdev = 0.022/0.022/0.022/0.000 ms
PING 127.0.0.1 (127.0.01) 56(84) bytes of data.
```

64 bytes from 127.0.01: icmp_req=1 ttl=64 time=0.020 ms
— 127.0.0.1 ping statistics —
1 packets transmitted, 1 received, 0% packet loss, time 0ms
rtt min/avg/max/mdev = 0.020/0.020/0.020/0.000 ms
From 127.0.0.1 icmp_seq=1 Destination Host Unreachable
— 127.0.0.2 ping statistics —
1 packets transmitted, 0 received, +1 errors, 100% packet loss, time 0ms

Notice that I started with the address that was not reachable first. When it pauses, the other thread starts immediately and kick-starts another thread. There is 0% packet loss on the first addresses that were pinged twice, however the first thread didn't complete until the end. Here is another type of thread that is slightly different.

```
>>> help('thread')
Help on built-in module thread:
NAME
thread
FILE
(built-in)
MODULE DOCS
http://docs.python.org/library/thread
DESCRIPTION
This module provides primitive operations to write multi-threaded programs.
The 'threading' module provides a more convenient interface.
CLASSES
__builtin__.object
lock
exceptions.Exception(exceptions.BaseException)
error
...
```

Ping test 2

```
#ping3.py
import os
import thread
num1=2
num2=1
```

```
dat="ping -c 1 127.0.0.%d" % num1
dat1="ping -c 1 127.0.0.%d" % num2
def mythread(t,x):
    a=os.system(x)
    print "thread %s" % t
    lock.release()
lock=thread.allocate_lock()
z=thread.start_new_thread(mythread, ("thread0",dat1,))
v=thread.start_new_thread(mythread, ("thread1",dat,))
```

Note we are using a different syntax to start the thread:

start_new_thread

start_new_thread(...)

start_new_thread(function, args[, kwargs])

(start_new() is an obsolete synonym)

We can add more arguments in the other script using a while loop. This script works but it will freeze due to the loop logic being equal to true. It can also lock up your computer depending on your computers performance capabilities. Lets take a look at the output.

```
python ping3.py
-1217881232
-1226269840
PING 127.0.01 (127.0.0.1) 56(84) bytes of data.
64 bytes from 127.0.0.1: icmp_req=1 ttl=64 time=0.025
ms
— 127.0.0.1 ping statistics —
1 packets transmitted, 1 received, 0% packet loss, time
0ms
rtt min/avg/max/mdev = 0.025/0.025/0.025/0.000 ms
thread thread1
PING 127.0.0.2 (127.0.0.2) 56(84) bytes of data.
From 126.0.0.1 icmp_seq=1 Destination Host Unreach-
able
— 127.0.0.2 ping statistics —
1 packets transmitted, 0 received, +1 errors, 100% packet
loss, time 0ms
thread thread0
^CTraceback (most recent call last):
File "ping4.py", line 20, in <module>
while 1: pass
```

```
KeyboardInterrupt
```

I had to manually break out before it locked up my system. It was interesting to watch my CPU shoot up to 100%, but it would have never exited because the while loop was true regardless of the results. This a logic error that has to do with iteration of 'z' and 'v'. The bottom line is that you can spend a great deal more time dealing with logic issues than actual threading issues.

A loop can also make things a little easier and cleaner. Keep the following in mind.

```
#ping4.py
import threading
def mythread(x):
    print 'Worker: %s' % x
    return
threads=[]
for i in range(3):
    t=threading.Thread(target=mythread,args=(i,))
    threads.append(t)
    t.start()
```

8. EasyGUI

8.1. EasyGUI

EasyGUI is the quick way to get a small program up and running with a nice interface. The goal of this book was to jump in and learn by doing. So far, we've created some simple programs very quickly using python programming language. EasyGUI allows you to program in a linear way and put up dialogs for input/output when needed. You can download 'easygui' from http://easygui.sourceforge.net/ or run ***"easy_install easygui"*** or run ***"pip install python-easygui"***.

The download page has a zip containing the 'easygui.py' and several other documents. The only document we need here is 'easygui.py'. Put this easygui.py file in the same directory where your scripts are located . The next step is to make sure you have Tkinter package installed. I use python-tk Tkinter to write 'Tk' applications with Python. It's helpful to think of EasyGUI as a bunch of functions or methods that act like wrappers to the 'Tkinter' toolkit meant to allow you to simplify and rapidly build GUI's without the knowledge of 'Tkinter' internals. Here is your first example:

```
#first.py first graphical app
from easygui import *
msgbox("Hello World. I like EasyGui")
```

Figure 8.1.: first.py

In two lines of code you have created a graphical message box 'msgbox'. If you were using 'Tkinter' directly, this would take a few more lines. Let's create another script with an image. Make sure you use a 'gif' image and not 'png' or 'jpg' which are not supported without python-pil (Python Image Library). You can install that library later and play with other image formats.

```
#second.py with image jandb.gif
from easygui import *
image="logo.gif"
msgbox("My new Logo",
ok_button="Enter", image=image)
```

Figure 8.2.: second.py

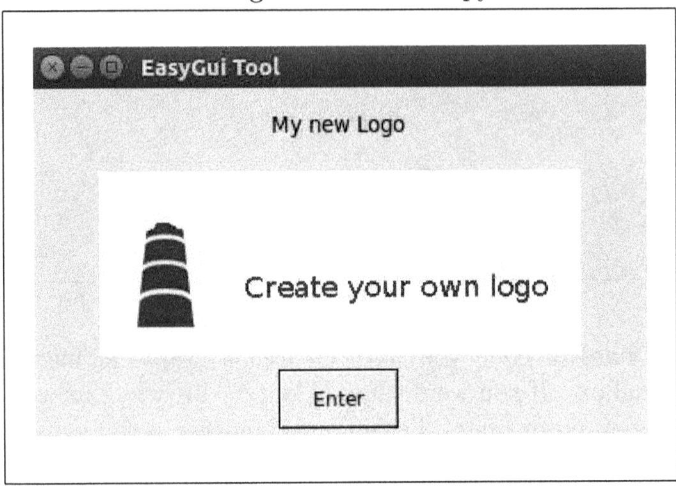

The best example would be the 'demo.py' that comes with easygui. If it's not there run the following code below:

```
#demo.py
from easygui import *
import sys

while 1:
    msgbox("Hello, world!")
    msg ="What is your favorite flavor?"
    title = "Ice Cream Survey"
    choices = ["Vanilla", "Chocolate", "Strawberry", "Rocky
Road"]
    choice = choicebox(msg, title, choices)

# note that we convert choice to string, in case
# the user canceled the choice, and we got None.
msgbox("You chose: " + str(choice), "Survey Result")

msg = "Do you want to continue?"
title = "Please Confirm"
if ccbox(msg, title): # show a Continue/Cancel dialog
    pass # user chose Continue
else:
```

sys.exit(0) # user chose Cancel

Figure 8.3.: demo.py

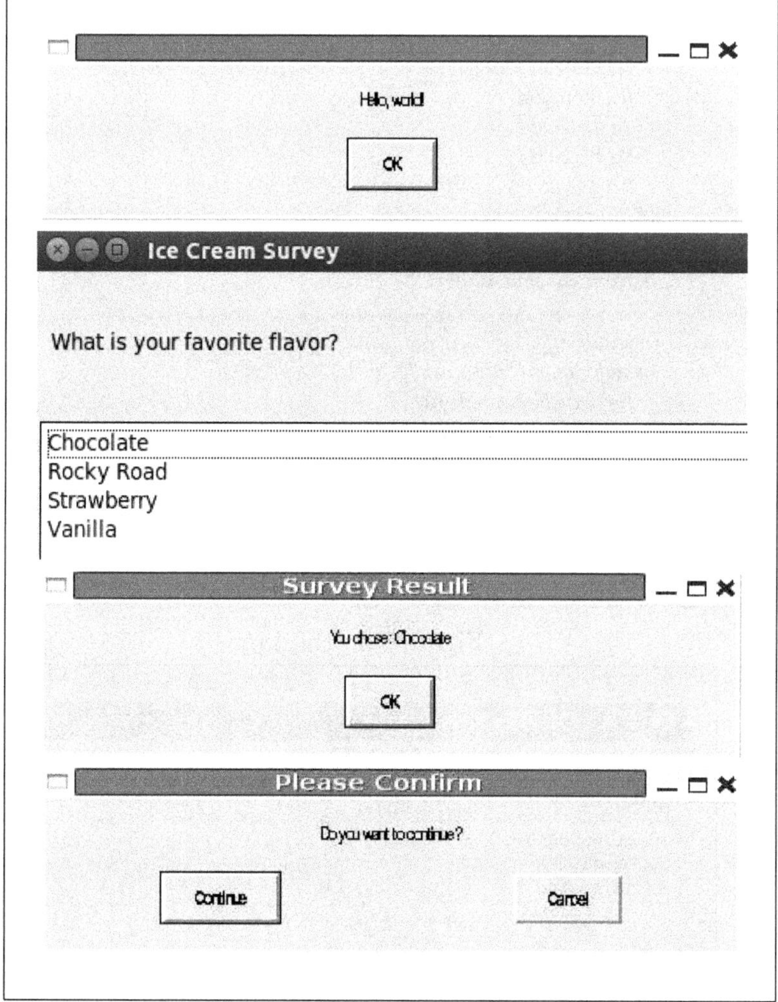

Notice that when you run the 'demo.py' it will also change the order of your 'choices=[]', you can fix this by being more creative in adjusting the choices. Such as: "choices=['A Vanilla', 'C Chocolate', 'B Strawberry', 'R Rocky Road']". To experience doing something more practical, we will create a 'csv' file to read from and call it 'data.csv'. It will contain the following:

```
#data.csv
0a,0b,0c,0d
1a,1b,1c,1d
2a,2b,2c,2d

#third.py
# call data.csv
from easygui import *

result=[]
blah=open("data.csv", "r")
for i in blah.readlines():
    result.append(i)
textbox("data", "title", result)
# don't forget you can still use console
print result
blah.close()
```

Figure 8.4.: third.py

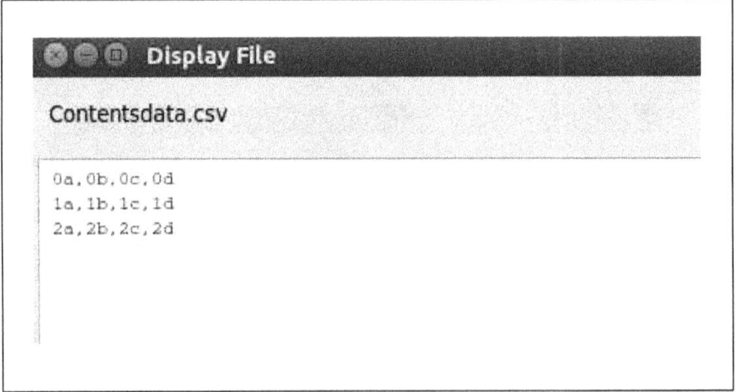

Also note that 'textbox' will word-wrap if the '.csv' file is too long. You can use 'codebox()' which does not wrap. You can also perform the same procedure without the loop as the file is essentially a list to begin with.

```
#fourth.py
from easygui import *
filename=("data.csv")
file=open(filename, "r")
text = file.readlines()
file.close()
codebox("Contents" + filename, "Display File", text)
```

So in summary. With the scripts listed including 'easygui' demo. You have enough to rapidly write basic GUI applications. The limitations you will discover are the uniqueness, design, type of boxes, appearance of buttons, box type, message locations, sizes, and fonts.

Now that you've seen EasyGui, you can weigh the limitations against the amount of code you would have to write to accomplish those tasks to achieve total creative control. For now, play and edit 'easygui.py' to change some of those fonts and features until you run into limitations. To demonstrate the lesson in a practice, import 'apartment.py' from the last chapter into our new program 'apt.py'. First let's review 'apartment3.py':

```
#apartment3.py
# required information:10 units with 2 bedrooms, 8 covered parking
#1 pool, x rooms, 15 people
class complex:
    def __init__(self, unit, parking, pool, rooms, people):
        self.unit=unit
        self.parking=parking
        self.pool=pool
        self.rooms=rooms
        self.people=people
    def calc(self):
        self.capacity=float(self.people)/self.rooms
        self.uncovered=100-(float(self.parking)/self.people*100)
```

```
            self.rooms=10*2
            self.freerooms=self.rooms-self.people
        def result(self):
            print "The complex is at %g capacity" % self.capacity
            print "There are %g percent people with uncovered parking" % self.uncovered
            print "We have %g rooms" % self.rooms
            print "We have %g free rooms left" % self.freerooms

    if __name__=="__main__":
        myCo=complex(10,8,1,20,15)
        myCo.calc() # these are tied together initialize
        myCo.result() # these are tied together
```

We need to add the if statement to run this program externally. To do this, you should first look to see that information being passed into the 'textbox' function is in the form of a list. Now, we need to change those print statements.

```
    #apartment4.py
    # required information:10 units with 2 bedrooms, 8 covered parking
    #1 pool, x rooms, 15 people
    class complex:
        def __init__(self, unit, parking, pool, rooms, people):
            self.unit=unit
            self.parking=parking
            self.pool=pool
            self.rooms=rooms
            self.people=people
        def calc(self):
            self.capacity=float(self.people)/self.rooms
            self.uncovered=100-(float(self.parking)/self.people*100)
            self.rooms=10*2
            self.freerooms=self.rooms-self.people
        def result(self):
            a="The complex is at %g capacity" % self.capacity
```

```
        b="There are %g percent people with uncovered
parking" % self.uncovered
        c="We have %g rooms" % self.rooms
        d="We have %g free rooms left" % self.freerooms
        data=[a,b,c,d]
        return data

if __name__=="__main__":
    myCo=complex(10,8,1,20,15)
    myCo.calc()
    for i in myCo.result():
    print i
```

We have the ability to integrate our program into our 'apt.py' EasyGUI program. For a clean presentation, let's add \n (newline) to each object in lists so that our data will be on separate lines.

```
#use and import apartment4.py
#apt.py
from apartment4 import *
from easygui import *

myCo=complex(10,8,1,20,15)
myCo.calc()
data=[]
for i in myCo.result():
    data.append(i+"\n")
textbox("apt data", "Apartment Complex", data)
```

Figure 8.5.: Apartment

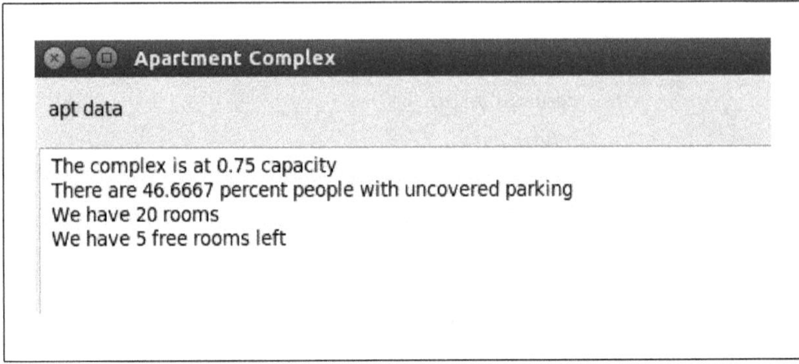

1. Imported both programs 'apartment.py' and 'easygui.py'
2. Initialize the program 'myCo'
3. Create a list data=[]
4. Populate the list with our loop statement
5. Add the data[] to our 'textbox'.

It takes six lines to integrate our program for graphical output. The only thing missing is a multi-enter box. Feel free to look into 'easygui' for this example listed below.

```
multenterbox(msg="Fill in values for the fields."
, title=" "
, fields=()
, values=()
)
```

For example:

```
msg = "Enter your personal information"
title = "Credit Card Application"
fieldNames = ["Name","Street Address","City","State","ZipCode"]
fieldValues = [] # we start with blanks for the values
fieldValues = multenterbox(msg,title, fieldNames)
```

Using the example above let's add it to our code 'extra.py'

```
#!/usr/bin/python
#use and import apartment4.py
```

```
#extra.py
from apartment4 import *
from easygui import *

msg="Enter Fields"
title="Apartment Complex"
fieldNames=["unit","parking","pool","rooms","people"]
fieldValues=[]

fieldValues=multenterbox(msg,title, fieldNames, fieldValues)
fd=fieldValues #print fd[0]
#myCo=complex(10,8,1,20,15)
myCo=complex(int(fd[0]),int(fd[1]),int(fd[2]),int(fd[3]),int(fd[4]))
myCo.calc()
data=[]
for i in myCo.result():
    data.append(i+"\n")
textbox("apt data", "Apartment Complex", data)
```

Figure 8.6.: Apartment input

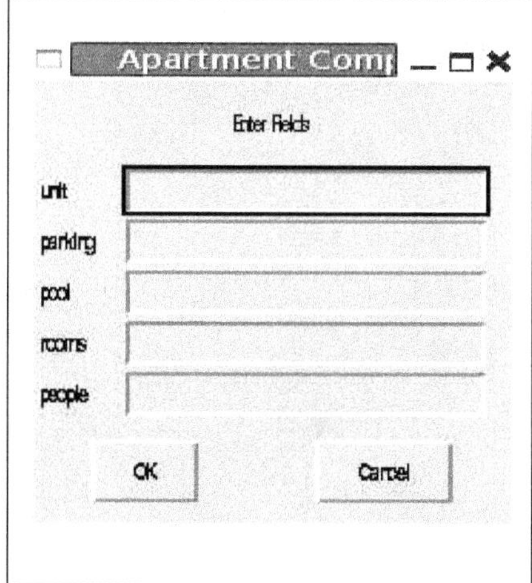

So in roughly '11' lines we added input fields for our apartment complex. You can find many other examples in the 'easygui.py' file. You can improve this code by wrapping 'fd=fieldValues' with 'int(fd)' and adding each field to 'complex()' You can also use a loop to populate those fields.

8.1.1. EasyGui Discontinued

Stephen Ferg retired the project in 2013 but it was picked up in later in 2014. Either way the framework is simple and not event driven. Get a copy of the code and feel free to make modifications of your choice.

8.1.2. Exercises

1. Calculate any two integers with 'easygui'.
2. Create a search and replace program for any integer, character, word using 'tkinter'.

9. Tkinter

9.1. Tkinter

As you have already discovered EasyGUI works really great for fast projects. Just about every piece of code you have written here and some that you are about to write can be easily modified for the EasyGUI interface with little effort. Now that you understand the basics of EasyGUI it just takes a little extra and you can start utilizing Tkinter directly with efficiency.

9.1.1. The Basics

A basic list

```
#food.py
list= ['milk', 'cheese', 'fruit', 'chicken']
print list
```

So here is our list of food items. To have it written to a 'Tk GUI' we import the library and wrap the code with the following lines:

```
#fooda.py
from Tkinter import *
root=Tk()
list= ['milk', 'cheese', 'fruit', 'chicken']
print list
root.mainloop()
```

Figure 9.1.: fooda.py

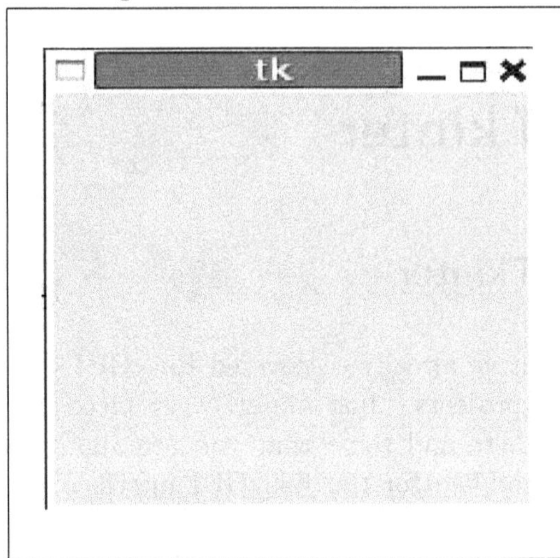

To close the program you will need to use your mouse and click the 'x' at the top right of the window you just created.

As you can see it didn't exactly display the items in the the window and it won't appear until the 'root.mainloop()' is executed. We need to prepare the data to be inserted into the 'X' display or window display.

```
#foodb.py
from Tkinter import *
root=Tk()
listb=Listbox(root)
listb.pack()
list= ['milk', 'cheese', 'fruit', 'chicken']
print list
root.mainloop()
```

Figure 9.2.: foodbb.py

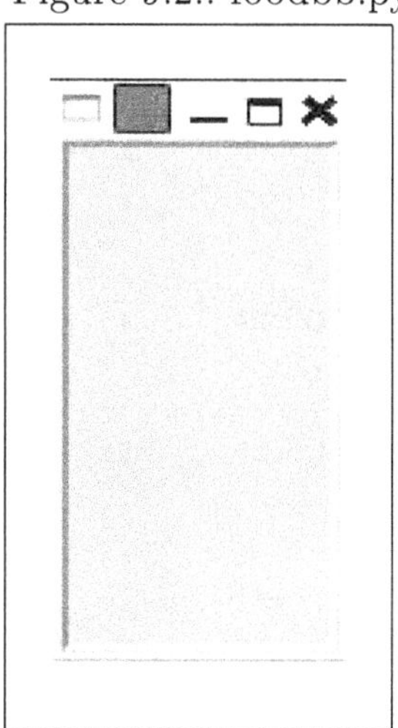

When you run this code you will notice a slight difference in appearance. There is a 'Listbox' inside the root window. The 'listbox.pack()' packs 'listbox' inside the root window to appear. All we need to do now is loop the list into 'listb.pack()'.

```
#foodc.py
from Tkinter import *
root=Tk()
listb=Listbox(root)
listb.pack()
list= ['milk', 'cheese', 'fruit', 'chicken']
for item in list:
    listb.insert(END, item)
print list
root.mainloop()
```

Figure 9.3.: foodc.py

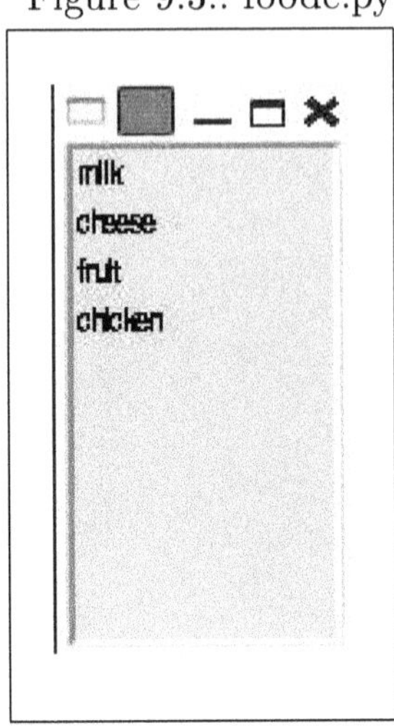

9.1.2. Simplify with functions

You now have a basic understanding of Tkinter and how to populate a 'listbox' using a list. You could do this a lot more easily using methods. For example:

```
# simple.py
from Tkinter import *
root=Tk()
def mbutton(mess):
    b=Button(root,text=mess)
    b.pack()
    b.mainloop()
mbutton("Press me")
```

Figure 9.4.: simple.py

This is a lot more refined and we can further extend this by adding a new method or extending the existing method.

```
#simplea.py
from Tkinter import *
root=Tk()
def mbutton(mess):
    b=Button(root,text=mess)
    b.pack()
def mlabel(lab):
    l=Label(root, text=lab)
    l.pack()
mbutton("Press me")
mlabel("My Python")
root.mainloop()
```

Figure 9.5.: simplea.py

Notice that we pulled the 'mainloop' out so both methods can utilize it. Let's extend this further with three methods.

```
#simpleb.py
from Tkinter import *
root=Tk()
def mbutton(mess):
    b=Button(root,text=mess)
    b.pack()
def mlabel(lab):
    l=Label(root, text=lab)
    l.pack()
def tbox():
    t=Text(root)
```

```
    t.pack()
mbutton("Press me")
mlabel("My Python")
tbox()
root.mainloop()
```

Figure 9.6.: simpleb.py

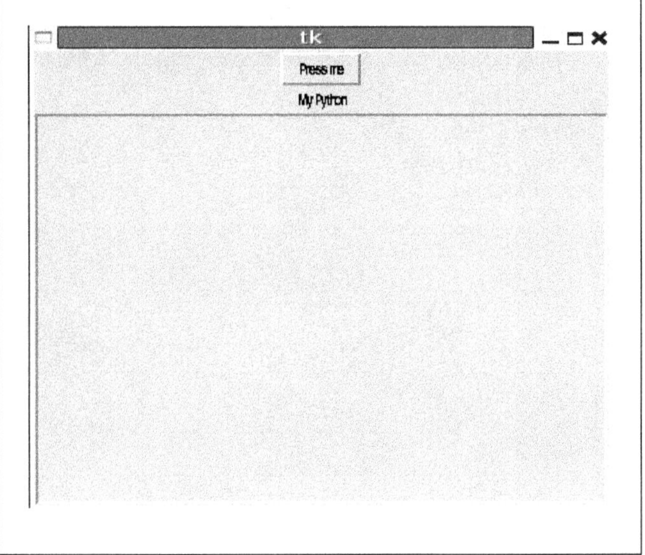

Next we should add data to a 'listbox'.

```
#simplec.py
from Tkinter import *
def mbutton(mess):
    b=Button(root,text=mess)
    b.pack()
def mlabel(lab):
    l=Label(root, text=lab)
    l.pack()
def tbox():
    t=Text(root)
    t.pack()
```

```
def lbox(list):
    lb=Listbox(root)
    lb.pack()
    for i in list:
        lb.insert(END, i)
root=Tk()
mbutton("Press me")
mlabel("My Python")
tbox()
lbox(['milk', 'cheese', 'fruit', 'chicken'])
root.mainloop()
```

Figure 9.7.: simplec.py

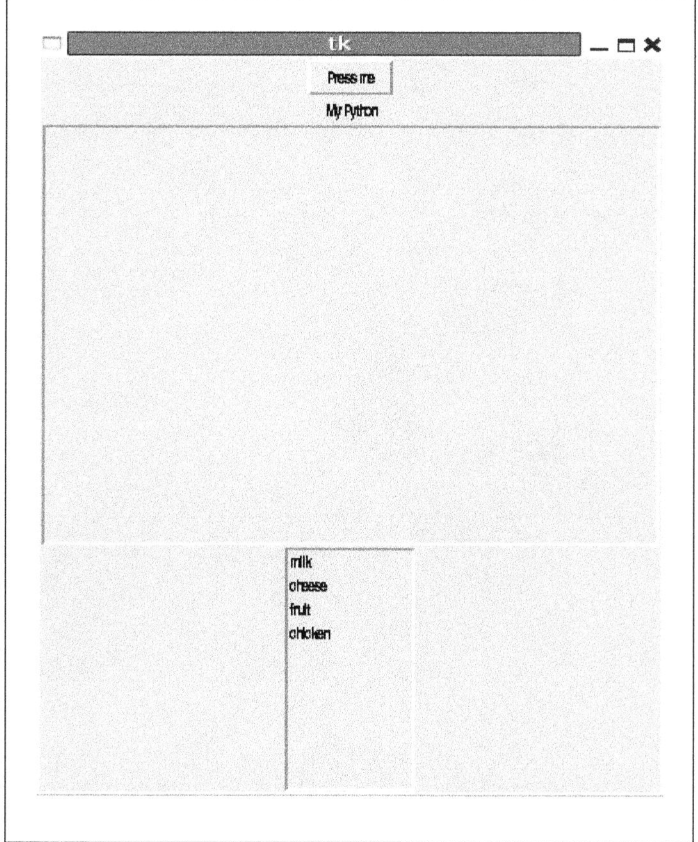

Notice that we moved 'root=Tk()' after the methods. This should give insight into the logic of how this program works. Let's actually use the button now and print some text with color. If you don't see 'asdf'. Run the program and type it in. You can type whatever you want.

```
#simpled.py
from Tkinter import *
def mlabel():
    l=Label(root, text='My Python repeating', fg='red')
    l.pack()
def mbutton(mess,m):
    b=Button(root,text=mess,command=m)
    b.pack()
def tbox():
    t=Text(root)
    t.pack()
def lbox(list):
    lb=Listbox(root)
    lb.pack()
    for i in list:
        lb.insert(END, i)
root=Tk()
mbutton("Press me",mlabel)
#mlabel("My Python")
tbox()
lbox(['milk', 'cheese', 'fruit', 'chicken'])
root.mainloop()
```

Figure 9.8.: simpled

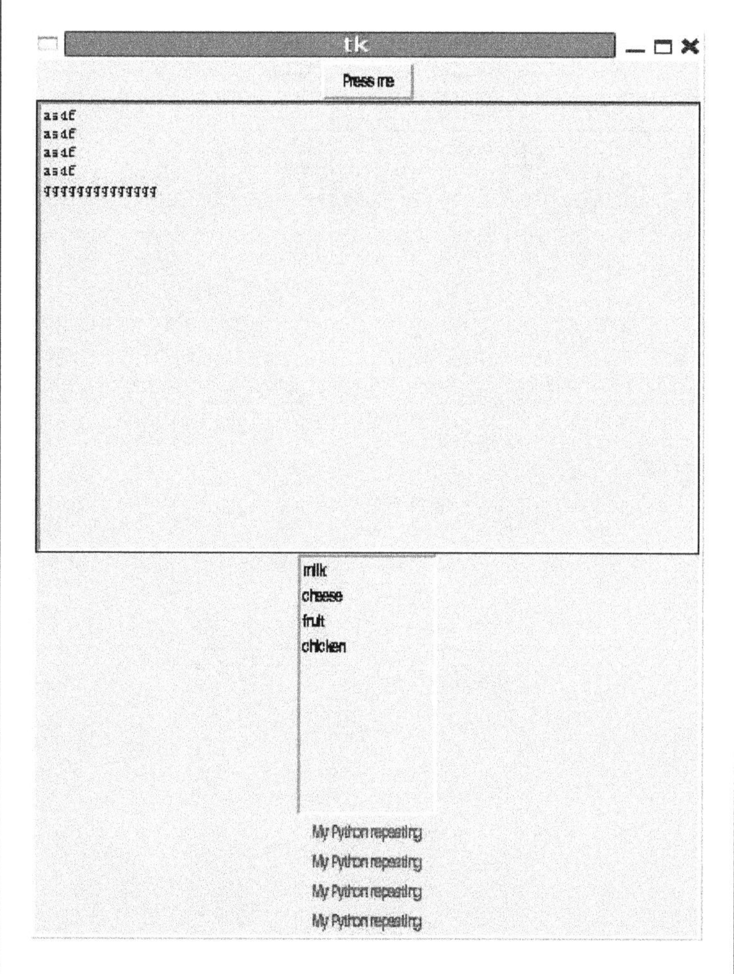

9.1.3. Widgets

At this point you should realize that pure Tkinter can be very flexible and offer an abundance of features for basic GUI programming. Here is a brief list of widgets that you can use.

Frame	*Label*	*Entry*
Text	*Canvas*	*Button*
Radiobutton	*Checkbutton*	*Scale*
Listbox	*Scrollbar*	*OptionMenu*
Spinbox	*LabelFrame*	*PanedWindow*

The properties of these widgets are specified in keyword arguments as you have already seen above such as root, text, command etc...

The widgets are positioned using geometry managers such as Place, Pack, and Grid. Actions are bound to events by resources. The resource is the keyword argument and command. Let take a look at some of the widgets:

```
#button.py
from Tkinter import *
root = Tk()
b= Button(root, text = 'python',command='', width =
'6', height='6',
activebackground='blue', bg='white', fg='red')
b.pack(padx = 20, pady=20)
root.mainloop()
```

Figure 9.9.: button.py

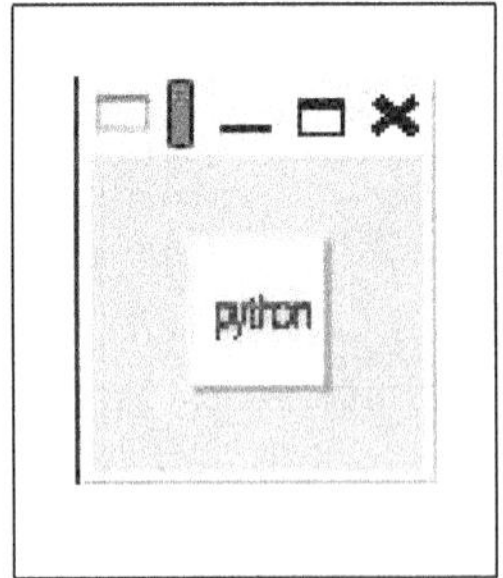


```
#canvas.py
from Tkinter import *
root=Tk()
```

```
c = Canvas(root, width='80', height = '60', bg='white')
c.pack (padx =5, pady=5)
s=c.create_line(10,30,10,30,40,10,20,45,30,80)
root.mainloop()
```

Figure 9.10.: canvas.py

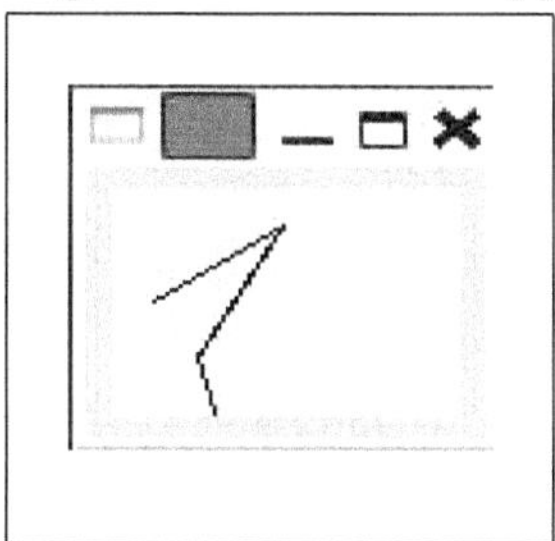

```
#canvaspic.py
from Tkinter import *
root=Tk()
c = Canvas(root, width='275', height='100', bg = 'white')
c.pack(padx=5, pady=5)
photo=PhotoImage(file='jandb.gif')
item=c.create_image(0,0, anchor=N+W,image=photo)
root.mainloop()
```

Figure 9.11.: canvaspic.py

```
#checkbutton.py
from Tkinter import *
root=Tk()
root.geometry('200x50+250+50')
check=Checkbutton(root,bg = 'white', text = 'Check 1',
font=('Helvetica',20))
check.pack()
root.mainloop()
```

Figure 9.12.: checkbutton.py

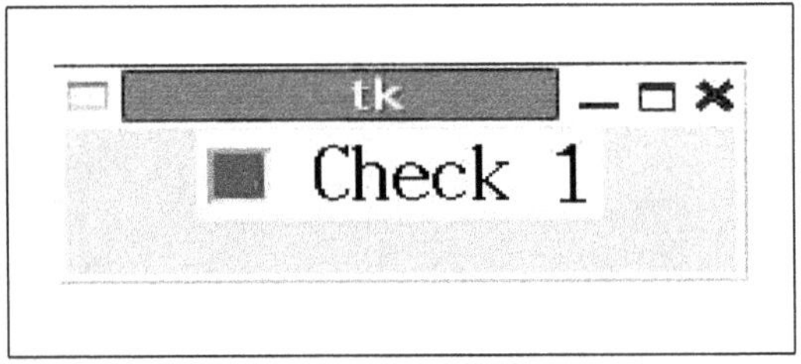


```
#entry.py
from Tkinter import *
root=Tk()
entry=Entry(root,bg='white').pack(padx=30,pady=10)
root.mainloop()
```

Figure 9.13.: entry.py

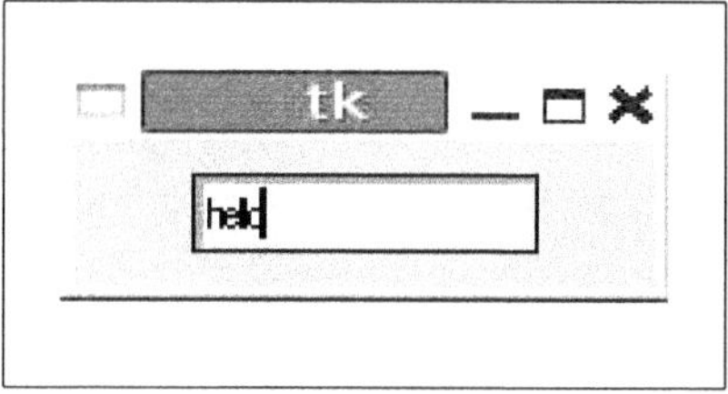

```
#frame.py
from Tkinter import *
root=Tk()
frame=Frame(root,bg='green', width=200, height=200)
frame.pack(padx=10,pady=10)
root.mainloop()
```

Figure 9.14.: frame.py

```
#lable.py
from Tkinter import *
root=Tk()
label=Label(root, font=("helvetica",15),fg='black', text='python
and tkinter')
```

```
label.pack(padx=10,pady=10)
root.mainloop()
```

Figure 9.15.: label.py

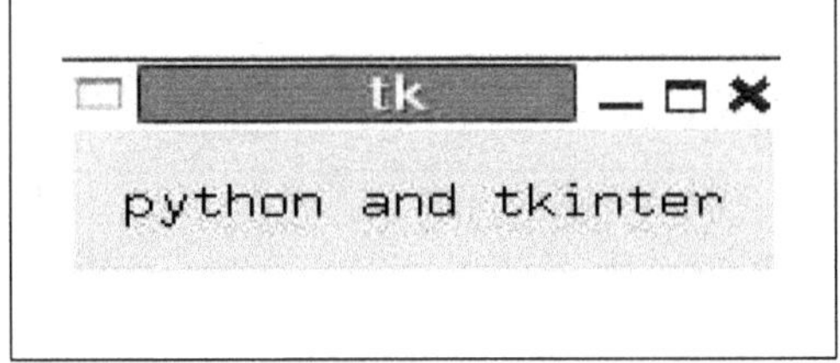


```
#listbox.py
from Tkinter import *
root=Tk()
l=Listbox(root,width=10)
l.pack(padx=10,pady=5)
list=['John','Jane','Doe']
for i in list:
    l.insert(END, i)
root.mainloop()
```

Figure 9.16.: listbox.py

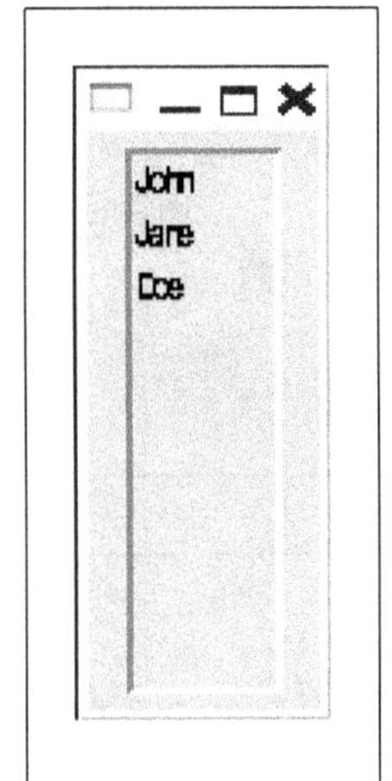

```
#menu.py
from Tkinter import *
root=Tk()
m=Menu(root)
filemenu=Menu(m,tearoff=0)
filemenu.add_command(label='Exit')
m.add_cascade(label='File', menu=filemenu)
root.config(menu=m)
root.mainloop()
```

Figure 9.17.: menu.py

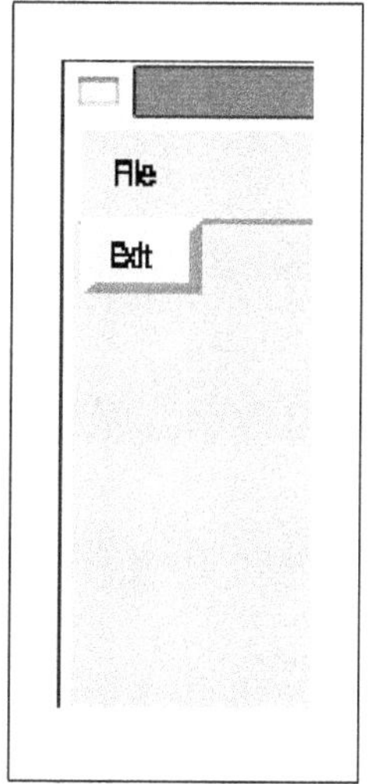


```
#scroll.py
from Tkinter import *
root=Tk()
f= Frame(root, bg='blue')
mscroll=Scrollbar(f, bg='green')
text = Text(f, width=20, height=10, yscrollcommand=mscroll.set)
mscroll.config(command=text.yview)
mscroll.pack(side = RIGHT, fill=Y)
text.pack()
f.pack()
root.mainloop()
```

Figure 9.18.: scroll.py

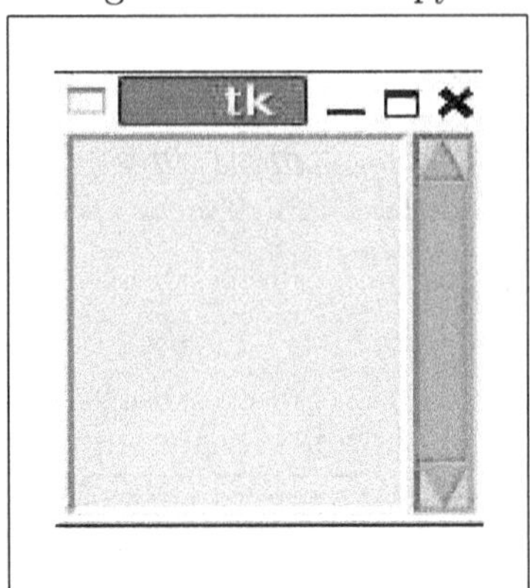

9.1.4. Entry widget in depth

Entry widget is a perfect example to demonstrate a thorough analysis of the widgets. This example will put it together piece by piece. It can also be used as a building block for password entry.

```
#ent.py
from Tkinter import *
root=Tk()
root.geometry('200x210+350+70')
ent=Entry(root, bg='white')
ent.pack()
button=Button(root, text='press me', command='')
button.pack()
listb=Listbox(root,bg='blue')
listb.pack()
root.mainloop()
```

Figure 9.19.: ent.py

The above are the building blocks for our program. An entry widget, a button widget, and a list box widget.

```
#ent1.py
from Tkinter import *
root=Tk()
root.geometry('200x210+350+70')
ent=Entry(root, bg='white')
#ent.pack()
ent.pack(anchor=W)
button=Button(root, text='press me', command='')
#button.pack()
button.pack(pady=20, anchor=E)
listb=Listbox(root,bg='blue')
listb.pack()
root.mainloop()
```

Figure 9.20.: ent1.py

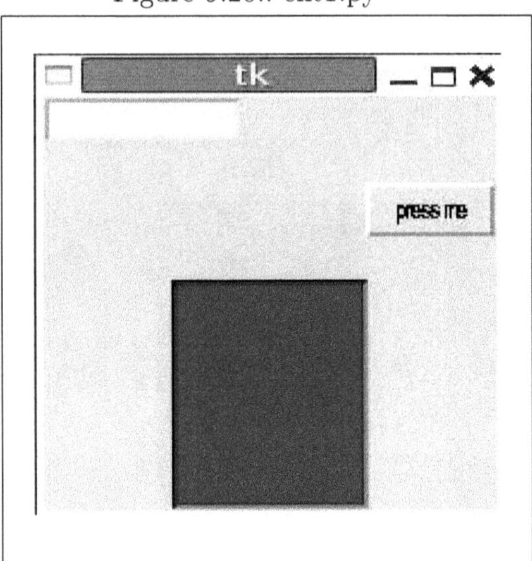

As you can see we can move our widgets and pad them using an x and y coordinate.

```
#ent2.py
from Tkinter import *

def myinsert(): #3
    name = ent.get()
    print name
    listb.insert(END,name)
    ent.delete(0,END)
root=Tk()
root.geometry('200x210+350+70')
ent=Entry(root, bg='white')
ent.pack(anchor=W)
button=Button(root, text='press me', command=myinsert)
button.pack(pady=20, anchor=E)
listb=Listbox(root,bg='blue')
listb.pack()
root.mainloop()
```

Figure 9.21.: ent2.py

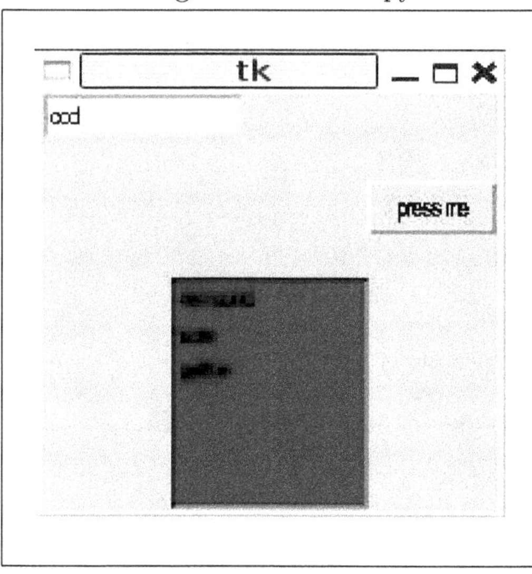

9.1.5. Practical Example

This next example uses the Tkinter grid geometry manager. Grid makes everything easier than using pack. Consider the following example:

<table>
<tr><td>label 1</td><td>Entry 1</td><td colspan="2" rowspan="2">Image</td></tr>
<tr><td>label 2</td><td>Entry 2</td></tr>
<tr><td></td><td></td><td>Button 1</td><td>Button 2</td></tr>
</table>

This type of configuration can be done easier with grid rather than pack. In the next example we will create a stock market calculator that I use every day.

9.1.5.1. Stock market Calculator prototype

The script will calculate potential profit based on the following: Quantity of shares purchased. Entry into market or cost to purchase shares and Exit or shares sold at specific price.

```
#stockproto.py
shares=raw_input("Enter quantity of shares: ")
entry=raw_input("Enter price per share: ")
exit=raw_input("Enter future exit price per share: ")
print "Cost to get in: $%f" % ( int(shares) * float(entry))
print "Exit: $%f" % ( int(shares) * float(exit))
profit = ( ( int(shares) * float(exit) ) - (int(shares) *
float(entry)) )
print "Profit: $%f" % profit
```

Results:

```
Enter quantity of shares: 1000
Enter price per share: .020
Enter future exit price per share: .030
Cost to get in: $20.000000
Exit: $30.000000
Profit: $10.000000
```

Now that we have our prototype complete. We will create an interface for the calculator.

```
#stockproto.py

from Tkinter import *

def myinsert():

    shares=e1.get()

    entry=e2.get()

    exit=e3.get()

    cost="Cost to get in: $%.2f" % ( int(shares) * float(entry))

    exitresult="Exit: $%.2f" % ( int(shares) * float(exit))

    profit=( (int(shares) * float(exit) ) - (int(shares) * float(entry)) )

    profitresult="Profit: $%.2f" % profit

    for item in [cost,exitresult,profitresult]:

        listb.insert(END,item)

def myclear():

    listb.delete(0,END)
```

```
root=Tk()
label=Label(root, text="Quantity Shares").grid(row=0)
label2=Label(root,text="Entry Price").grid(row=1)
label3=Label(root,text="Exit Price").grid(row=2)
e1=Entry(root,bg='white')
e2=Entry(root,bg='white')
e3=Entry(root,bg='white')
e1.grid(row=0,column=1)
e2.grid(row=1,column=1)
e3.grid(row=2,column=1)
button=Button(root, text='calculate', command=myinsert)
button.grid(row=3,column=1)
clearb=Button(root, text="clear",command=myclear)
clearb.grid(row=3,column=0)
listb=Listbox(root,bg='light blue')
listb.grid(row=4,column=1, padx=20,pady=20)
root.mainloop()
```

Figure 9.22.: Stock Spread Calculator

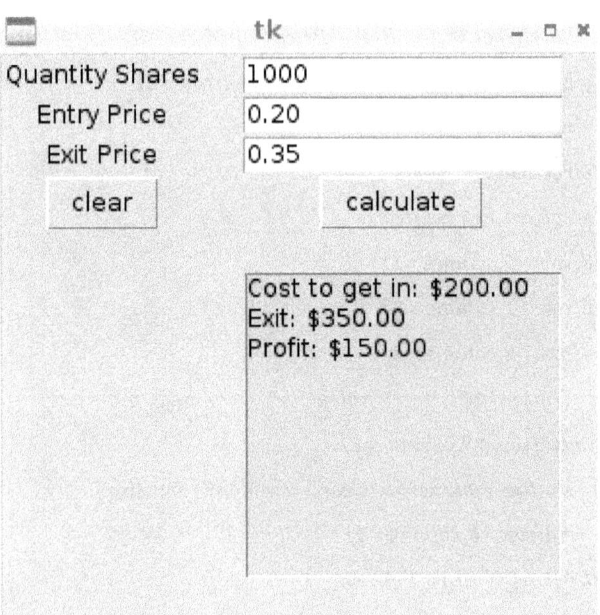

When you are ready to create other projects please keep in mind that it's easier to work with the code between 'root=Tk' and mainloop as displayed below before adding other calculations.

root=Tk()
...
...
root=mainloop()

The 'button' command points to the two methods to either 'get()' and perform the calculations from the prototype and populate the listbox or clear contents in the list box.

9.1.6. Exercises

Same as previous chapter except use Grid instead of pack. Grid is best

10. WxWidgets

10.1. Wx-widgets

WxWidgets is a widely supported and portable GUI API. It has some similarities to Tkinter but it is far more comprehensive and rich. WxWidgets relies heavily on OOP. Download at http://wxpython.org and follow the instructions for installation. Please do not download 'wx3.0'. Search for 'wx2.8'. This chapter supports an older version of Wx-widgets to be compatible with 'PythonCard' in the next section.

Here is a quick list of the widget objects to get you started:

Base Widgets

- wx.Window
- wx.Control
- wx.ControlWithItem
- Top Level Widgets
- wx.Frame
- wx.MDIParentFrame
- wx.MDIChildFrame
- wx.Dialog
- wx.PopupWindow

Containers - containers contain other widgets known as children widgets

- wx.Panel
- wx.Notebook
- wx.ScrolledWindow
- wx.SplitterWindow

Dynamic Widgets

These are widgets edited by users.

- wx.Button
- wx.BitmapButton
- wx.Choice
- wx.ComboBox
- wx.CheckBox
- wx.Grid
- wx.ListBox
- wx.RadioBox
- wx.RadioButton
- wx.ScrollBar
- wx.SpinButton
- wx.SpinCtrl
- wx.Slider
- wx.TextCtrl
- wx.ToggleButton

Static Widgets - These widgets display information not edited by user.

- wx.Gauge
- wx.StaticText
- wx.StaticBitma- wx.StaticLine
- wx.StaticBox

Then you have widgets for Menu, status and tool bar. These are the primary widget objects you will use in your application development.

- wx.MenuBar
- wx.ToolBar
- wx.Statusbar

The first step is to import 'wx'.

```
>>>import wx
>>>help('wx')

Help on package wx:
NAME
wx
FILE
/usr/lib/python2.6/dist-packages/
wx-2.6-gtk2-unicode/wx/__init__.py
MODULE DOCS
http://docs.python.org/library/wx
DESCRIPTION
```

```
#--------------------------------------------------------------
---.
# Name: __init__.py
# Purpose: The presence of this file turns this directory
into a
# Python package.
#
# Author: Robin Dunn
#
# Created: 8-Aug-1998
# RCS-ID: $Id: __init__.py,v 1.11 2005/06/02 03:31:17
RD Exp $
# Copyright: (c) 1998 by Total Control Software
# Licence: wxWindows license
#--------------------------------------------------------------
---.
PACKAGE CONTENTS
__version__
_animate
_calendar
_controls
_controls_
_core
_core_
_gdi
_gdi_
_gizmos
_glcanvas
_grid
_html
_media
_misc
_misc_
_stc
_webkit
_windows
_windows_
_wizard
_xrc
animate
build (package)
calendar
xrc
etc...
```

Lets create a window

```
#firstwx.py
import wx
app=wx.App()
frame=wx.Frame(None, -1, 'first')
frame.Show()
app.MainLoop()
```

Here is a structured way to create our first 'wx' application. Let's migrate this to a class.

```
#secondwx.py
import wx
class Blah(wx.App):
    def OnInit(self):
        frame=wx.Frame(None, -1, "I love python")
        frame.Show(True)
        self.SetTopWindow(frame)
        return 1
app=Blah()
app.MainLoop()
```

The 'wx.Frame' is our constructor container with three arguments, None for parent window, identifier -1 for window and a title "I love python". Next we need our frame to be shown and the window to be a top level window. If this function executes correctly it will have a value of '1'. The next step is to initialize the "class: aap=Blah()", we also need to loop it 'app.MainLoop()'.

Let's re-factor the code further using 'PySimpleApp()': Note this class might be deprecated, but it will still work.

```
>>> help('wx.PySimpleApp')
Help on class PySimpleApp in wx:
wx.PySimpleApp = class PySimpleApp(App)
 | A simple application class. You can just create one of these
and
 | then then make your top level windows later, and not have
to worry
 | about OnInit. For example::
 |
 | app = wx.PySimpleApp()
 | frame = wx.Frame(None, title='Hello World')
 | frame.Show()
 | app.MainLoop()
 |
```

```
| :see: `wx.App`
|
| Method resolution order:
| PySimpleApp
| App
| PyApp
| EvtHandler
| Object
| __builtin__.object
|
| Methods defined here:
|
| OnInit(self)
|
| __init__(self, redirect=False, filename=None, useBestVisual=False, clearSigInt=True)
| :see: `wx.App.__init__`
|
| ----------------------------------------------------------------------
| Methods inherited from App:
|
| Destroy(self)
|
| MainLoop(self)
| Execute the main GUI event loop
|
| RedirectStdio(self, filename=None)
| Redirect sys.stdout and sys.stderr to a file or a popup window.
|
| RestoreStdio(self)
|
| SetOutputWindowAttributes(self, title=None, pos=None, size=None)
```

Refactoring code:

```
#thirdwx.py
import wx
class Blah(wx.Frame):
    def __init__(self,x,y,z):
        wx.Frame.__init__(self,x,y,z)
app=wx.PySimpleApp()
frame=Blah(x=None, y=-1,z="wow")
frame.Show()
app.MainLoop()
```

Add a button:

```
#fourthwx.py
import wx
class Blah(wx.Frame):
    def __init__(self,x,y,z):
        wx.Frame.__init__(self,x,y,z)
        panel=wx.Panel(self)
        button=wx.Button(panel,label="press me")
app=wx.PySimpleApp()
frame=Blah(x=None, y=-1,z="wow")
frame.Show()
app.MainLoop()
```

Get the button to do something like close the Frame.

```
#fifthwx.py
import wx
class Blah(wx.Frame):
    def __init__(self,x,y,z):
        wx.Frame.__init__(self,x,y,z)
        panel=wx.Panel(self)
        button=wx.Button(panel,label="press me")
        self.Bind(wx.EVT_BUTTON,self.closebutton,button)
    def closebutton(self,event):
        self.Close(True)
app=wx.PySimpleApp()
frame=Blah(x=None, y=-1,z="wow")
frame.Show()
app.MainLoop()
```

10.1.1. PythonCard

It can be very tedious to develop a GUI application without an Integrated Development Environment (IDE). Below are three IDE's that support python:

1. Open Komodo
2. PyQT
3. Eclipse

Eclipse is a very popular IDE primarily used for Java or C programming. It supports WxWidgets and python. Should your application reach a high level of complexity, you might find yourself using Eclipse. Because Eclipse is beyond the scope of this book, I would like to instead introduce PythonCard. PythonCard is a GUI construction kit that uses the Python language. 'The PythonCard motto is: "Simple things should be simple and complex things should be possible."

The goal with this book as with PythonCard's motto is to develop graphical applications quickly. PythonCard separates the presentation from the application logic by using a resource file to define the presentation using dictionaries. The application logic is a separate python file. This allows the developer to concentrate on application logic rather then tedious aspects of the widgets size, position, color, and feature. To get started with our first application, download "PythonCard" from http://pythoncard.sourceforge.net

```
#pcard1.py
from PythonCard import model
class blah(model.Background):
    pass
if __name__=="__main__":
    app=model.Application(blah)
    app.MainLoop()
```

Now if you try to run the script, you will get an error because you need to create a resource file using "resourceEditor".

Figure 10.1.: pycard template

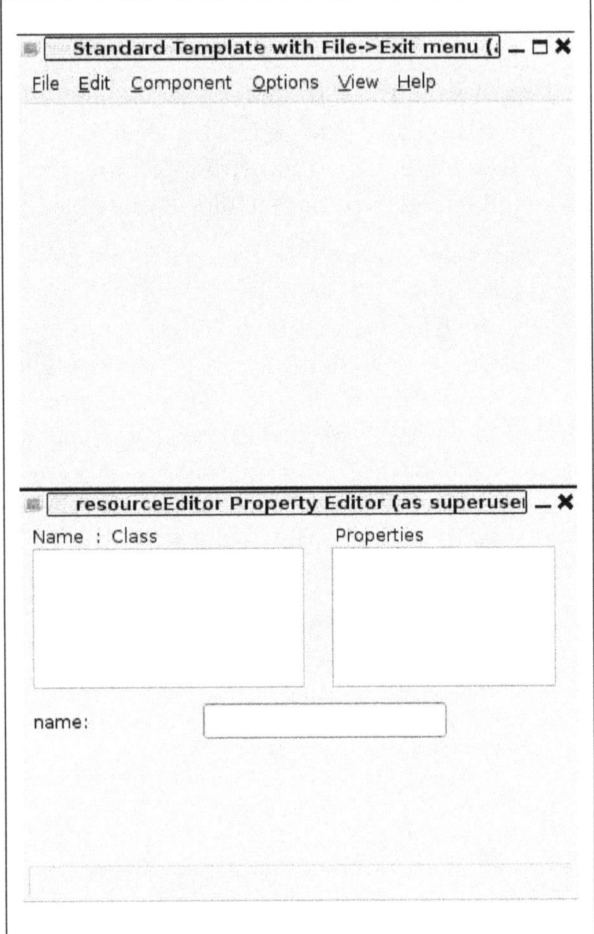

Like the samples you can select a Component and choose TextField. Save the file as 'pcard1.rsrc.py'. When you run 'pcard1.py', a window should display with your newly added TextField entry.

The application class is where we define a method for each event you wish to handle. The method name is important as it determines which block of code is executed. The form of method name is on_(component_name)_(event name).

Here is a list of components

- BitmapCanvas
- Button
- Calendar
- CheckBox
- Choice
- CodeEditor
- ComboBox
- Gauge
- Grid
- HtmlWindow
- IEHtmlWindow
- Image
- ImageButton
- List
- MultiColumnList
- Notebook
- PasswordField
- RadioGroup
- Slider
- Spinner
- StaticBox
- StaticLine
- StaticText
- TextArea
- TextField
- ToggleButton
- Tree

The events are automatically bound to each component and are as follows:

- gainFocus
- loseFocus
- mouseContextDoubleClick
- mouseContextDown
- mouseContextUp
- mouseDoubleClick
- mouseDown
- mouseDrag

- mouseEnter
- mouseLeave
- mouseMiddleDoubleClick
- mouseMiddleDown
- mouseMiddleUp
- mouseMove
- mouseUp
- timer
- mouseClick
- closefield
- keyPress

Attributes such as 'backgroundcolor', command string, font, 'foregroundColor', name position, size, 'toolTip', and visible exist for each component. PythonCard has over "65+" application examples with the installation package including a samples file that lists all of them at once.

10.1.2. PythonCard Application

PythonCard is a graphical WYSIWYG tool to develop a WxWidget interface for your project. It is the 'resourceEditor' that creates an XML file with the correct coordinates for each widget such as text field, button etc... You leverage the PythonCard API by passing your data into each method as a dictionary file. Let's create our first pythoncard application. We will start with a simple script.

```
# basic file write
#bfile.py
def FileWrite(d):
    f=open('file.txt','a')
    f.write(d)
    f.close()
if __name__=='__main__':
    d=raw_input("enter something: ")
    FileWrite(d)
```

In the example above, we are using raw_input to write something to a file. It is important to verify everything step-by-step. Beliow is a test script to verify that the file will write properly.

```
#test.py
from bfile import *
d=raw_input('enter something: ')
FileWrite(d)
```

When we run this script, we should see that the data entered appears in the 'file.txt'. Next, we import this into our new application.

```
#app.py
from PythonCard import model
from bfile import *
class Minimal(model.Background):
    # pass
    def on_bsubmit_mouseClick(self, event):
        namef = str(self.components.fname.text)
        namel = str(self.components.lname.text)
        self.components.stest.text=' '
        FileWrite(namef)
        FileWrite(namel)
        self.components.fname.text=' ' # clear text field
        self.components.lname.text=' ' # clear
        self.components.stest.visible=1
        self.components.stest.text=namef
if __name__ == '__main__':
    app = model.Application(Minimal)
    app.MainLoop()
```

Run the **resourceEditor** program and create an event method. The key is to assign a component to 'namef' and 'namel'. The file write is not evident in the application like it is when done behind the scenes. We have two other components for the text field. The last two components become visible after the 'bsubmit' button is clicked. When you build the method, the widget name gets changed to 'on_bsubmit_mouseClick'. Note that the application writes to the 'file.txt' behind the scenes.

Figure 10.2.: pcard apartment complex list

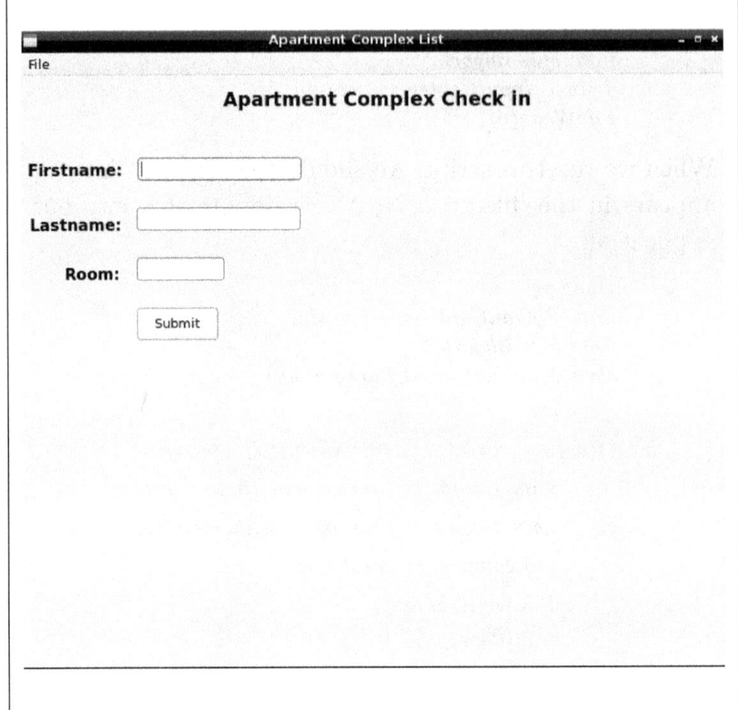

In the image to the right of the Firstname: field there is a StaticText called 'stest' that is not visible by default. We are doing everything with all the components.

We are assigning (self.components.fname.text) to 'namef'...

Here is the resource file:
{'application':{'type':'Application',
'name':'Minimal',
'backgrounds': [
{'type':'Background',
'name':'bgMin',
'title':'Apartment Complex List',
'size':(729, 639),
'menubar': {'type':'MenuBar',
'menus': [
{'type':'Menu',

```
'name':'menuFile',
'label':'File',
'items': [
{'type':'MenuItem',
'name':'menuFileExit',
'label':'E&xit\tAlt+X',
'command':'exit',
},
]
},
]
},
'components': [
{'type':'StaticText',
'name':'stest',
'position':(318, 85),
'text':'StaticText',
'visible':False,
},
{'type':'Button',
'name':'bsubmit',
'position':(120, 231),
'label':'Submit',
},
{'type':'StaticText',
'name':'sroom',
'position':(45, 189),
'font':{'style': 'bold', 'faceName': u'Sans', 'family': 'sansSerif',
'size': 12},
'text':'Room:',
},
{'type':'TextField',
'name':'room',
'position':(120, 181),
},
{'type':'StaticText',
'name':'title',
'position':(210, 13),
'font':{'style': 'bold', 'faceName': u'Sans', 'family': 'sansSerif',
'size': 14},
'text':'Apartement Complex Check in',
},
{'type':'TextField',
'name':'lname',
'position':(120, 128),
'size':(170, 31),
},
{'type':'StaticText',
'name':'slname',
'position':(9, 140),
'font':{'style': 'bold', 'faceName': u'Sans', 'family': 'sansSerif',
'size': 12},
'text':'Lastname:',
```

```
},
{'type':'StaticText',
'name':'sfame',
'position':(7, 85),
'font':{'style': 'bold', 'faceName': u'Sans', 'family': 'sansSerif',
'size': 12},
'text':'Firstname:',
},
{'type':'TextField',
'name':'fname',
'position':(121, 78),
'size':(170, 31),
},
] # end components
} # end background
] # end backgrounds
} }
```

10.1.3. Summary:

Even with an IDE, you can spend a lot of time in Wx-widgets, making your application more presentable and complex. With PythonCard you have plenty of examples to use and reuse. PythonCard meets our criteria for rapid application development and portability.

11. Sockets and Databases

11.1. socket programming

Python has several modules which give access to the application layer such as FTP, HTTP, Telnet, SSH, etc. There are times when you need to implement your own application layer protocol. To do this we use (sockets).

```
>>>help('socket')
DESCRIPTION
This module provides socket operations and some related functions.
On Unix, it supports IP (Internet Protocol) and Unix domain sockets.
On other systems, it only supports IP. Functions specific for a
socket are available as methods of the socket object.
Functions:
socket() - create a new socket object
socketpair() - create a pair of new socket objects [*]
fromfd() - create a socket object from an open file descriptor [*]
gethostname() - return the current hostname
gethostbyname() - map a hostname to its IP number
gethostbyaddr() - map an IP number or hostname to DNS info
getservbyname() - map a service name and a protocol name to a port number
getprotobyname() - map a protocol name (e.g. 'tcp') to a number
ntohs(), ntohl() - convert 16, 32 bit int from network to host byte order
htons(), htonl() - convert 16, 32 bit int from host to network byte order
inet_aton() - convert IP addr string (123.45.67.89) to 32-bit packed format
inet_ntoa() - convert 32-bit packed format IP to string (123.45.67.89)
ssl() - secure socket layer support (only available if configured)
socket.getdefaulttimeout() - get the default timeout value
```

socket.setdefaulttimeout() - set the default timeout value
create_connection() - connects to an address, with an optional timeout
[*] not available on all platforms!

11.1.1. TCP sockets

Lets begin with the TCP server. The sample code below is the client. It is important that you run the server before testing the client file. You must have both files for the code to function properly.

```
#tcpc.py
import socket
HOST = 'localhost'
PORT = 8001
s = socket.socket(socket.AF_INET, socket.SOCK_STREAM)
s.connect((HOST, PORT))
data = s.recv(1024)
s.close()
```

The remote host is “host=localhost”, so in this case our host is local. The port is 8001 on the remote server and the socket platform is unix inet, sock stream or DGRAM for datagram. The following example uses stream. Now, we need a connect object to bind to the host/port and recv 1024 bits. We can then watch as our data streams into the buffer. Now, we close the object. Below is the server:

```
#tcps.py
import socket
HOST = '127.0.0.1'
PORT = 8001
s = socket.socket(socket.AF_INET, socket.SOCK_STREAM)
s.bind((HOST, PORT))
s.listen(1)
conn, addr = s.accept()
print 'Connected by', addr
conn.close()
```

The difference here is that we are using bind object to bind an IP address to a port number. We are using the accept object and assigning it to the 'addr' variable and then we are sending an acknowledgement.

- Run python 'tcps.py' server first.
- Then open up another terminal or command prompt and run 'tcpc.py' the client program.

The server will print that it received a connection from ('127.0.0.1', 444xx) or something similar from the client port data stream. This is not really practical for our purposes. Let's send back some data by adding something to the client. To do this, add the following to the last line print 'Received', repr(data).

Now startup the server 'tcps.py' again and see the results when you connect with the client (see below). You have not really received data yet. The server needs to send it. For this to happen, we need to add a send object to the server.

```
#tcpc1.py
import socket
HOST = 'localhost'
PORT = 8001
s = socket.socket(socket.AF_INET, socket.SOCK_STREAM)
s.connect((HOST, PORT))
data = s.recv(1024)
s.close()
print 'Received', repr(data)
```

Now when you fire up the server and connect with the client, you will notice that client prints that it received an acknowledgement. To further test your code, have the client send something to the server. If you see "socket address in use", you might want to close the previous server application and restart the server again.

```
#tcpc2.py
import socket
HOST = 'localhost'
PORT = 8001
s = socket.socket(socket.AF_INET, socket.SOCK_STREAM)
s.connect((HOST, PORT))
s.send('Hello, world')
data = s.recv(1024)
s.close()
print 'Received', repr(data)
```

But first we must modify the server to receive that data.

```
#tcps2.py
import socket
HOST = '127.0.0.1'
PORT = 8001
s = socket.socket(socket.AF_INET, socket.SOCK_STREAM)
s.bind((HOST, PORT))
s.listen(1)
conn, addr = s.accept()
print 'Connected by', addr
data=conn.recv(1024)
conn.send('Acknowledge')
print data
conn.close()
```

So now we have our client and server applications talking to each other in an efficient manner. However, a loop may work a bit better on the server if a stream of data is to be sent.

```
#tcps3.py
import socket
HOST = '127.0.0.1'
PORT = 8001
s = socket.socket(socket.AF_INET, socket.SOCK_STREAM)
s.bind((HOST, PORT))
s.listen(1)
conn, addr = s.accept()
print 'Connected by', addr
while 1:
    data= conn.recv(1024)
    if not data: break
    conn.send(data)
conn.close()
```

The client is as follows:

```
#tcpc3.py
import socket
HOST = 'localhost'
PORT = 8001
s = socket.socket(socket.AF_INET, socket.SOCK_STREAM)
s.connect((HOST, PORT))
while 1:
    data=raw_input("Text: ")
    if not data:
        break
```

```
        else:
            s.send(data)
            print "sent message:", data
    s.close()
```

When you run it, the server won't disconnect as long as the client is sending a data stream. For example here is the data stream that I entered:

```
Text: wow
send message: wow
Text: working
send message: working
Text: cool
send message: cool
Text:
```

So the client is sending a stream of data and printing the result of sent data to the screen. Though two print statements might be overkill, how do we really know for sure that data is being sent? To verify this, we add a print statement to the server.

```
#tcps4.py
import socket
HOST = '127.0.0.1'
PORT = 8001
s = socket.socket(socket.AF_INET, socket.SOCK_STREAM)
s.bind((HOST, PORT))
s.listen(1)
conn, addr = s.accept()
print 'Connected by', addr
while 1:
    data= conn.recv(1024)
    if not data: break
    conn.send(data)
    print "sent: " , data
conn.close()
```

Now the server will print out data that has been sent and break the server when the connection stream is lost. We can also add an exception for a graceful exit. (This is done to avoid an error in the TCPIP 3 way handshake data stream.)

11.1.2. UDP sockets

UDP sockets are not that different really. The exception is the three way handshake. With TCP you need TCP header flags for SYN, SYN/ACK, and ACK. UDP is less reliable but has advantages in other areas of network communication. It will send the data regardless of acknowledgement. The following is a UDP server:

```
#server.py
from socket import *
host = "localhost"
port = 8001
buf = 1024
addr = (host,port)
u= socket(AF_INET,SOCK_DGRAM)
u.bind(addr)
while 1:
    data,addr = u.recvfrom(buf)
    if not data:
        break
    else:
        print "Received message:", data
u.close()
```

The client is as follows:

```
#client.py
from socket import *
host = "localhost"
port = 8001
buf = 1024
addr = (host,port)
u= socket(AF_INET,SOCK_DGRAM)
msg= "Send messages to server: ";
print "Message sent:", msg
while (1):
    data = raw_input('Text: ')
    if not data:
        break
    else:
        if(u.sendto(data,addr)):
```

```
            print "send message:",data
        u.close()
```

Notice that this UDP data stream closes without an error. This is because it doesn't have a 3 way handshake like TCPIP sockets. You now have enough information to build applications that utilize a network connection.

11.2. Database SQLite

SQLite is one of the most convenient and quick ways to prototype and build a SQL database. However keep in mind SQLite is more powerful then people realize. It can compete very easily with MySQL or Postgress for small datasets. It also has the advantage of being light weight and portable. All concepts here can be applied to MySQL and Postgress very easily.

11.2.1. SQLite Primer

Visit http://www.sqlite.org and download the latest binary for your system. The following is an example of creating '3' fields in a database called 'mytable.db'. The table is called 'foo'.

```
./sqlite3 mytable.db
SQLite version 3.6.10
Enter ".help" for instructions
Enter SQL statements terminated with a ";"
sqlite> create table foo (id INTEGER PRIMARY KEY,
fname VARCHAR(50), lname VARCHAR(50));
sqlite> insert into foo values (1,'john','doe');
sqlite> select * from foo
...> ;
1|john|doe
sqlite>
```

As you can see, it's very simple. Also note that I forgot the semicolon in "select * from foo". I had to enter it on the next line. Below are the list of commands to use.

```
sqlite> .help
.bail ON|OFF Stop after hitting an error. Default OFF
.databases List names and files of attached databases
.dump ?TABLE? ... Dump the database in an SQL text
format
.echo ON|OFF Turn command echo on or off
.exit Exit this program
.explain ON|OFF Turn output mode suitable for EXPLAIN
on or off.
.header(s) ON|OFF Turn display of headers on or off
.help Show this message
.import FILE TABLE Import data from FILE into TABLE
.indices TABLE Show names of all indices on TABLE
.load FILE ?ENTRY? Load an extension library
.mode MODE ?TABLE? Set output mode where MODE is
one of:
csv Comma-separated values
column Left-aligned columns. (See .width)
html HTML <table> code
insert SQL insert statements for TABLE
line One value per line
list Values delimited by .separator string
tabs Tab-separated values
tcl TCL list elements
.nullvalue STRING Print STRING in place of NULL values
.output FILENAME Send output to FILENAME
.output stdout Send output to the screen
.prompt MAIN CONTINUE Replace the standard prompts
.quit Exit this program
.read FILENAME Execute SQL in FILENAME
.schema ?TABLE? Show the CREATE statements
.separator STRING Change separator used by output mode
and .import
.show Show the current values for various settings
.tables ?PATTERN? List names of tables matching a LIKE
pattern
.timeout MS Try opening locked tables for MS milliseconds
.timer ON|OFF Turn the CPU timer measurement on or off
.width NUM NUM ... Set column widths for "column" mode
sqlite>
```

We can look at the description of the table using ".sechma".

```
./sqlite3 mytable.db
SQLite version 3.6.10
Enter ".help" for instructions
Enter SQL statements terminated with a ";"
sqlite> .schema
CREATE TABLE foo (id INTEGER PRIMARY KEY,
fname VARCHAR(50), lname VARCHAR(50));
sqlite>
```

We can easily export the data as follows:

```
sqlite> .mode csv
sqlite> .output data.csv
sqlite> select * from foo;
sqlite> .quit
/home/knoppix:$ cat data.csv
1,john,doe
```

To further emphasize the power of SQLite, you can execute queries at the command line.

```
./sqlite3 mytable.db "select * from foo;"
```

Results:

```
1|john|doe
```

This feature makes SQLite very robust. You can quickly script something in bash or AWK. You can also import 'OS' or 'System' to access the application externally and use languages such as Perl, Python, 'C', or 'C++'. Libraries are also available so that you don't have to call the program externally.

11.2.2. Python SQLite

As of version 2.6 SQLite library is included in core python package. Let's create another table called user.db similar to our primer above.

```
#create.py
# create user.db
import sqlite3
con = sqlite3.connect('user.db')
cur = con.cursor()
cur.execute('CREATE TABLE userinfo (id INTEGER
PRIMARY KEY, fname VARCHAR(20),
lname VARCHAR(30))')
con.commit() # comment back
cur.execute('INSERT INTO userinfo (id, fname, lname)
VALUES(NULL, "john", "doe")')
con.commit()
cur.execute('SELECT * FROM userinfo')
print cur.fetchall()
```

To list a record:

```
#record.py
# list information in table
import sqlite3
con=sqlite3.connect('user.db')
cur=con.cursor()
cur.execute('SELECT * FROM userinfo')
print cur.fetchall()
```

To add a new record:

```
#record1.py
# list information in table
import sqlite3
con=sqlite3.connect('user.db')
cur=con.cursor()
cur.execute('insert into userinfo(id,fname,lname) VALUES(NULL, "george", "peterson")')
con.commit()
cur.execute('SELECT * FROM userinfo')
print cur.fetchall()
```

To update a record:

```
#update.py
# list information in table
import sqlite3
con=sqlite3.connect('user.db')
cur=con.cursor()
cur.execute("update userinfo set lname='bob' where fname='george'")
con.commit()
cur.execute('SELECT * FROM userinfo')
print cur.fetchall()
cur.close()
con.close()
```

Notice the last line closes the cursor and the connection.

11.2.3. Exercises

1. Create a really simple chat server with sockets
2. Create family address book with names, phone numbers, addresses, etc...

12. CGI, W SGI Framework Development

12.1. CGI

CGI is the quick and dirty way to bring your applications to the web. The "Common Gateway Interface" (CGI) is an Internet standard that defines how web server software generates pages using a programming language or scripting languages. Perl was the most common scripting language used for this. However nearly any language can be used. Most languages have libraries that can use the CGI, but even a Unix bash script can be used to build pages. For instructions on how to setup Apache on Mac visit this url: http://www.cgi101.com/book/connect/mac.html. For windows or linux visit http://www.apache.org

Below is an example of a bash script:

```
#!/bin/bash
echo "Content-type: text/html\n"
echo "<html>"
echo "<p>Hello world"
echo "</html>"
```

Here is an example of a python script:

```
#!/usr/bin/python
#firstweb.py
print 'Content-type: text/html\n\n'
print "hello world"
```

The primary thing here is "Content-type" and "print" statement. In Apache Web server you can place your files in the 'cgi-bin' directory to execute. You can also rename your files with the '.pl' extension which is Perl's default extension for 'cgi-bin' applications. If you have access to apache "httpd.conf', you need to add the extension to the #'AddType' handler such as:

#AddType application/x-httpd-pl .py .pyc

The '.py' or '.pyc' will allow you to execute your python applications in '/cgi-bin' directory. Test to make sure you can execute your application using "chmod +ax script.py." Below is an example of using a variable.

```
#secweb.py
print 'Content-type: text/html\n\n'
var="Hello world"
print """
<html><head>
<title>Second Web Page</title>
</head><body>
<h1> Messasge to you: %s</h1>
</body>
</html>
""" % var
```

Notice also that I place most everything within the quotes print """ """ % var. Here is an example of a simple form.

```
#form.py
print "Content-type:text/html\n\n"
print """
<html>
<form action="pform.py" method="get">
First Name: <input type="text" name="fname"> <br>
Last Name: <input type="text" name="lname">
<input type="submit" value="Submit">
</form>
"""
```

However you can leave the above form in a regular HTML file. Make sure you call the correct file in the action statement ***action="pform.py"*** or ***action="/cgi-bin/pform.py"***. All of these examples assume you are in the 'cgi-bin' directory. To do the actual work, you would use another file to retrieve the stored values in a form.

```
#pform.py
import cgi,cgitb
form=cgi.FieldStorage()
#get data from fields
firstname=form.getvalue('fname')
lastname=form.getvalue('lname')
print "Content-type:text/html\n\n"
print """
<html>
<h1>Entries from form</h1>
<p>First name is: %s
<p>Last name is: %s
<hr>
</html>
""" % (firstname,lastname)
```

Notice the import cgi,cgitb and FieldStorage() function.

```
>>>help('cgi')
Help on module cgi:
NAME
cgi - Support module for CGI (Common Gateway Interface)
scripts.
FILE
/usr/lib/python2.6/cgi.py
MODULE DOCS
http://docs.python.org/library/cgi
DESCRIPTION
This module defines a number of utilities for use by CGI
scripts
written in Python.
CLASSES
UserDict.UserDict
FormContentDict
FormContent
SvFormContentDict
InterpFormContentDict
FieldStorag
...
```

Here is the cgitb

```
>>>help('cgitb')
Help on module cgitb:
NAME
cgitb - More comprehensive traceback formatting for Python
scripts.
FILE
/usr/lib/python2.6/cgitb.py
MODULE DOCS
http://docs.python.org/library/cgitb
```

```
DESCRIPTION
To enable this module, do:
import cgitb; cgitb.enable()
at the top of your script. The optional arguments to enable()
are:
display - if true, tracebacks are displayed in the web browser
logdir - if set, tracebacks are written to files in this directory
context - number of lines of source code to show for each
stack frame
format - 'text' or 'html' controls the output format
By default, tracebacks are displayed but not saved, the con-
text is 5 lines
and the output format is 'html' (for backwards compatibility
with the
original use of this module)
Alternatively, if you have caught an exception and want cgitb
to display it
for you, call cgitb.handler(). The optional argument to han-
dler() is a
3-item tuple (etype, evalue, etb) just like the value of sys.exc_info().
The default handler displays output as HTML.
CLASSES
Hook
class Hook
...
```

Very simply, we pull values from the form and assign them to a variable. Here is an example of retrieving a user name and password.

```
#form2.py
print "Content-type:text/html\n\n"
print """
<html>
<form action="pform2.py" method="get">
Username: <input type="text" name="username"> <br>
Password: <input type="text" name="password">
<input type="submit" value="Submit">
</form>
"""
```

It might be best to change password type="hidden". Make this change and process the form again.

```
#pform2.py
import cgi,cgitb
#form=cgi.FieldStorage()
#get data from fields
mypass="jppass"
def webpage(username,password):
```

```
    print """
    <html>
    <h1>Entries from form</h1>
    <p>First name is: %s
    <p>Last name is: %s
    <hr>
    </html>
    """ % (username,password)
def login():
    print "Content-type:text/html\n\n"
    form=cgi.FieldStorage()
    if form.has_key("username") and form.has_key("password"):
        token=form["password"].value
    if (token==mypass):
        webpage(form["username"].value,form["password"].value)
    else:
        print "<h1>Wrong username or password!!!</h1>"
login()
```

You will notice new methods inherited from 'UserDict' method form.has_key(self,key). I assigned it to variable token. If the value of "mypass == token" then the webpage() method will be processed with an 'else' statement "Wrong username or password!!!" Things to note: Cookies and sessions are not included in this chapter. I'm not partial to writing cookies to deal with the session management of web pages. I find that when I get to that point in writing code, I might as well migrate to a web framework like Django, which is included in this book. You have the option to apply minimal cryptographic data encoding such as base64.

Example:

```
decode=base64.b64decode('encoded_string')
```

To encrypt:

```
#crypt.py
import base64
print base64.b64encode("mypassword")
```

To decrypt:

```
#decrypt.py
import base64
print base64.b64decode('bXlwYXNzd29yZA==')
```

If I wanted to use this in an enterprise environment, I might configure using crypt library for stronger security. I would store my cipher passwords in an SQLite database and my sessions would be controlled by the python random library coupled with 'username' and authenticated once. I would then carry the arguments for 'username' and bind a session to each page. I thought about using part of the password as a session coupled with random() to add increased security for the weakness of the random() library. If you have arrived at that point in development, perhaps you should choose a web framework that manages authentication solution such as Django.

12.2. WSGI

According to Python Enhancement Program (PEP) 333. A Web Server Gateway Interface (WSGI) works by using callbacks. The application utilizes a function to call a request: application(environ, start_response)

1. environ - This is a Python dictionary with CGI defined environment variables including "wsgi.input" for POST variables.
2. start_resonse - a callback to return HTTP headers.
3. start_response(status, response_headers, exc_info=None)
    a) status - This is an HTTP status string
    b) response_headers - contains 2 tuples , headers and key values.
    c) exc_info - exception handling

For example:

```
#first.py
from cgi import *
def hello(environ, start_response):
    start_response('200 OK', [('Content-Type', 'text/html')])
    return ["<p>Hello World, and good day!!!</p>"]
if __name__ =="__main__":
    from wsgiref.simple_server import make_server
    srv = make_server('localhost', 8080, hello)
    srv.serve_forever()
```

Yes it seems strange at first but it's designed to meet a wide range of potential frameworks and servers. The start_response writes the data to the output screen as follows: **"python first.py"**

Open up a browser and visit the site using the following link: http://127.0.0.1:8080

```
localhost.localdomain - - [09/Mar/2011 16:09:59] "GET
/favicon.ico HTTP/1.1" 200 35
localhost.localdomain - - [09/Mar/2011 16:10:02] "GET
/favicon.ico HTTP/1.1" 200 35
localhost.localdomain - - [09/Mar/2011 16:10:02] "GET
/ HTTP/1.1" 200 35
```

The key thing to note here is the stand-alone server wsgiref:

```
help('wsgiref')
wsgiref - wsgiref – a WSGI (PEP 333) Reference Library
FILE
/usr/lib/python2.6/wsgiref/__init__.py
MODULE DOCS
http://docs.python.org/library/wsgiref
DESCRIPTION
Current Contents:
* util – Miscellaneous useful functions and wrappers
* headers – Manage response headers
* handlers – base classes for server/gateway implementa-
tions
* simple_server – a simple BaseHTTPServer that supports
WSGI
* validate – validation wrapper that sits between an app and
a server
to detect errors in either
* handlers – base classes for server/gateway implementa-
tions
* simple_server – a simple BaseHTTPServer that supports
WSGI
```

```
    * validate - validation wrapper that sits between an app and
a server
    to detect errors in either
    To-Do:
    * cgi_gateway - Run WSGI apps under CGI (pending a
deployment standard)
    * cgi_wrapper - Run CGI apps under WSGI
    * router - a simple middleware component that handles URL
traversal
    ...
```

For a more practical method, let's create another framework with a variable.

```
#hello.py
from cgi import *
def hello(environ, start_response):
    par= parse_qs(environ.get('QUERY_STRING', ''))
    if 'aname' in par:
        aname= escape(par['aname'][0])
    else:
        aname= 'World'
    start_response('200 OK', [('Content-Type', 'text/html')])
    return ["<p>Hello %(aname)s!</p>" % {'aname':aname}]
if __name__ == '__main__':
    from wsgiref.simple_server import make_server
    srv = make_server('localhost', 8080, hello)
    srv.serve_forever()
```

In this scenario we set query to the "par" variable and plan to return that variable in the form of a dictionary. We can now visit the site at the following address:

http://127.0.0.1:8080/?aname=William

The hard reality is that it's relatively easy to write a WSGI application but exceptionally difficult and tedious to write a framework. You would have to think of many things including a URL handler. If it is necessary to write code for every single URL (every page, file, media) , regular expressions would help. You would need to write an interface to the server for load, memory, port, and a 'middlware' to deal with exception handling, request and preprocessing, and last but not least, debugging issues. You will also need some sort of template system, or all your HTML will be encapsulated in python code. Media integration is also an important because 'wsgi' doesn't deal with media very well. It's recommended that you let a webserver such as Apache handle media files. Examples of web frameworks using WSGI PEP 333 are Django, CherryPy, and Pylons.

It should be stated that python has a great deal more frameworks out there including: Zope, Quixote, Webware, SkunkWeb and more. Each of these frameworks have their own middleware.

12.2.1. Creating a Web framework

Below is a rudimentary scaffolding of a bit of code I called "raspberrypi web framework". Currently it's missing middleware, ORM and additional error handling features. Additional information about this can be found at:

http://github.com/thecount12/raspberryweb.

It's a great jump start to building a web framework from scratch. A significant block of code below is commented out. It's an example of how to utilize the class.

```
import re
import traceback
from jinja2 import Template
from jinja2 import Environment, FileSystemLoader, Pack-
ageLoader
e = Environment(loader=FileSystemLoader('~/raspberryweb/templates'))
#template=Template('Hello {{ name}}!')
from cgi import parse_qs,escape

class Raspberry:
    """raspberry web framwork.
    example:
    class application(Raspberry):
        urls = [
    ("/", "index"),
```

```
("/hello/(.*)","hello"),
("/jinja/(.*)","jinja"),
("/tmpl/(.*)","tmpl"),
("/tmpl2/(.*)","tmpl2")
]
    def GET_index(self):
        return "Main Page"
    def GET_hello(self, name):
        return "Hello, %s!" % name
    def GET_jinja(self,name):
        return str(template.render(name="John Doe"))
    def GET_tmpl(self,name):
        Rtemplate=e.get_template('mytemplate.html")
        return str(Rtemplate.render())
    def GET_tmpl2(self,name):
        Rtemplate=e.get_template('mytemp2.html')
        dict={'name':'will','last':'gunn'} #{{dict}} in tem-
plate
        return str(Rtemplate.render(dict=dict))

template/
mytemp2.html
{% if dict %}
<p>{{dict}}
<p>{{dict.name}}
<p>{{dict.will}}
{%endif%}
    """

    def __init__(self, environ, start_response):
        self.environ = environ
        self.start = start_response
        self.status = "200 OK"
        self._headers = []
    def header(self, name, value):
        self._headers.append((name, value))
    def __iter__(self):
        try:
```

```
            x = self.delegate()
            self.start(self.status, self._headers)
        except:
            headers = [("Content-Type", "text/plain")]
            self.start("500 Internal Error", headers)
            x = "Internal Error:\n\n" + traceback.format_exc()
        # return value can be a string or a list. we should be
able to
        # return an iter in both the cases.
        if isinstance(x, str):
            return iter([x])
        else:
            return iter(x)
    def delegate(self):
        path = self.environ['PATH_INFO']
        method = self.environ['REQUEST_METHOD']
        for pattern, name in self.urls:
            m = re.match('^' + pattern + '$', path)
            if m:
                # pass the matched groups as args
                args = m.groups()
                funcname = method.upper() + "_" + name
                func = getattr(self, funcname)
                return func(*args)
        return self.notfound()
    def webinput(self,key):
        data=parse_qs(self.environ['QUERY_STRING'])
        item=data.get(key,[''])[0] # (key,[]) return list same
key
        return escape(item)
    def webpost(self):
        try:
            rbodysize=int(self.environ.get('CONTENT_LENGTH',0))
        except (ValueError):
            rbodysize=0
```

```
        request_body=self.environ['wsgi.input'].read(rbodysize)
        d=parse_qs(request_body)
        return d
    def webformat(self,data,key):
            item=data.get(key,[''])[0]
            return escape(item)

class application(Raspberry):
    thehtml=""" <html><form method="post">
    <p>fname: <input type="text" name="fname">
    <p>lname: <input type="text" name="lname">
    <p><input type="submit" value="Submit"></form>
    </html>
    """
    urls = [
        ("/", "index"),
        ("/hello/(.*)","hello"),
        ("/jinja/(.*)","jinja"),
        ("/tmpl/(.*)","tmpl"),
        ("/tmpl2/(.*)","tmpl2"),
        ("/storage/(.*)","storage"),
        ("/storage2/(.*)","storage2"),
        ("/mypost/","mypost"),
        ("/mypost2/","mypost2")
        ]
    def GET_index(self):
        return "Main Page"
    def GET_hello(self, name):
        return "Hello, %s!" % name
    def GET_jinja(self,name):
        return str(template.render(name="John Doe"))
    def GET_tmpl(self,name):
        Rtemplate=e.get_template('mytemplate.html')
        return str(Rtemplate.render())
    def GET_tmpl2(self,name):
```

```
        Rtemplate=e.get_template('mytemp2.html')
        dict={'name':'will','last':'gunn'} #{{dict}} in template
        return str(Rtemplate.render(dict=dict))
    def GET_storage(self,name):
        d=parse_qs(self.environ['QUERY_STRING'])
        print d
        print "asdf: %s" % d.get('id',[''])[0]
        print "fort: %s" % d.get('foo',[''])[0]
        return "Storage, %s" % name
    def GET_storage2(self,name):
        f=self.webinput('id')
        print f
        return "hello %s" % f
    def GET_mypost(self):
        return self.thehtml
    def POST_mypost(self): # error if GET does not exist
first
        try:
            rbodysize=int(self.environ.get('CONTENT_LENGTH',0))
        except (ValueError):
            rbodysize=0
        request_body=self.environ['wsgi.input'].read(rbodysize)
        d=parse_qs(request_body)
        print d
        return "strange"
    def GET_mypost2(self):
        return self.thehtml
    def POST_mypost2(self):
        res=self.webpost()
        print res
        firstname=self.webformat(res,'fname')
        lastname=self.webformat(res,'lname')
        print firstname
        print lastname
        return "interesting"
```

```
if __name__ == '__main__':
    from wsgiref import simple_server
    httpd = simple_server.make_server('192.168.1.126', 8080,
application)
    try:
        httpd.serve_forever()
    except KeyboardInterrupt:
        pass
```

12.2.2. Summary

Creating web frameworks is both rewarding and challenging. These are some features included in frameworks.

- Paste or equivalent
- ORM - SQLAlchemy
- Forms function
- Improved Template feature
- /static/ development for media such as CSS and Javascript
- Cache
- threading
- memory managment

12.2.3. Exercises

1. Substitute base64 with md5
2. Substitute SQLite with MySQL
3. create 'username' and password authentication using a form and store authentication credentials in a database.

13. Django

13.1. Django

You have learned quite a bit in the last few chapters about python and the web. This chapter focuses on building a comprehensive web site rapidly without the crux and nuisance of repeating repetitive programming tasks that often accompany the creation and maintenance of a web site. To achieve this goal a Web Framework is needed. Plenty of web frameworks exist for python. They are often referred to as Content Management Frameworks (CMF), or interpreted as Content Management Systems (CMS).

Django uses a Model-View-Controller (MVC), which is a method for developing software by defining and accessing data via a model, but separate from request and routing logic. This model is also separate from the user interface or (view).

MVC allows the components to be loosely coupled. A developer can change the URL for a given part of the application without effecting the underlying implementation. A designer can change a page's HTML without

having to touch the Python code that renders it. And a database 'admin' can rename a database table and specify the change in a single place rather than having to run search and replace for dozens of files.

13.1.1. Setting up django

Using a Debian based flavor of Linux like Ubuntu, you can get the packages by using apt package manager. Type the following command: ***apt-get install python-django***. If you are running a Mac OS type: ***pip install Django***

You will need to be root to run for the command above to work.

All site development should be done outside of Apache. Integration of Apache will come at the end of the tutorial.

13.1.2. start project

To create a directory name that will contain the project data, first type in the following command:

django-admin.py startproject fooblah

The directory fooblah will contain 4 files.

1. __init__.py: place holder for python modules
2. manage.py: to fire up services
3. settings.py: implied
4. urls.py: path, search using regular expressions

Then run the following in the "fooblah" directory:

python manage.py runserver

This will start Django framework on port 8000. By default you can visit: ***http://127.0.0.1:8000/***

Changing ports or IP 's can be accomplished as follows: Before you run the command, you do need to know the IP address for your computer. Your IP address will be different than the one you see below.

python manage.py runserver 8080

python manage.py runserver 192.168.1.1:8000

13.1.3. Create a view

The next step is to create a view. Typically the name would be 'views.py', but it can be any name. The content of the file is what is important. In the 'fooblah' directory. Type the following command: ***python manage.py startapp blah***

Go into the "blah" directory and open views.py and add the following:

```
#views.py
from django.http import HttpResponse
def hello(request):
    return HttpResponse("My new web view")
```

Now open settings.py in "fooblah" directory and add "blah" to INSTALLED_APPS as follows:

```
INSTALLED_APPS = (
'django.contrib.admin',
'django.contrib.auth',
'django.contrib.contenttypes',
'django.contrib.sessions',
'django.contrib.messages',
'django.contrib.staticfiles',
'django.contrib.flatpages',
'django.contrib.sites',
'blah',
)
```

The next step is to edit urls.py in the "fooblah" directory.

```
#urls.py
from blah.views import hello
#add just below (r'^admin/' etc... don't forget comma
","
url('^hello/$', hello),
```

Note that we are matching '^hello' to function 'hello'. To see your page, open ***http://localhost:8000/hello*** in your browser. If you go to any other directory you will get a 404 error. Let's add something to the root site and create the following functions.

```
#views.py
def newroot(request):
    return HttpResponse("oh wow")
#urls.py
from blahsite.views import newroot
url('^$',newroot),
```

13.1.4. Dynamic content: datetime()

To make the site more dynamic, we will make some modifications to the existing files.

```
#views.py
import datetime
def mydate(request):
    now = datetime.datetime.now()
    html = "<html><body>The current time is %s.</body></html>"
% now
    return HttpResponse(html)
#urls.py
from blahsite.views import mydate
('^mytime/$', mydate),
```

Feel free to visit the site ***http://localhost:8000/mytime***. The problem is that this is still hard coded and not very flexible for rapid changes. We need to allow designers the opportunity to change the HTML pages without knowledge of python.

13.1.5. Templates

I like to test my template locally first before handing the code over to web designers. Once complete they can make adjustments to the HTML, JS or CSS.

```
#views.py
from django.template import Template, Context # tem-
platemydate
def templatemydate(request):
    now=datetime.datetime.now()
    t=Template("<html><body>It is now {{ tempdate
}}.</body></html>")
    html=t.render(Context({'tempdate': now}))
    return HttpResponse(html)
#urls.py
from fooblah.views import templatemydate
('^tempdate/$',templatemydate),
```

13.1.6. Free HTML development

We are nearly at a point where your graphic designer can have complete creative freedom to design the site. The designer will need to access and adjust 'base.html' template. In essence this functions like an HTML template.

You need to edit settings.py and change the following tag under "TEMPLATES = ["

```
'DIRS': [],
'DIRS': [os.path.join(BASE_DIR,'django_templates')],
```

You also need to create a directory called 'django_templates' which will contain your new HTML files. This will need to be in the root of your site. In this example make sure the new directory is in 'fooblah' directory.

```
#base.html
<html>
<body>
<center><h1>This is my base.html file</h1></center>
I can enter all kinds of strange stuff here
<p>
{% block content %} {% endblock %}
</body></html>
```

Any python related information would be found in within: ***{% block content %} {% endblock %}***.

```
#date2.html
{% extends "base.html" %}
{% block content %}
it is now {{ thedate }}.
<b>
<p>
<pre>
calculalte 2+2={{ mcalc}}
</pre>
{% endblock %}
```

Now create a view for 'date2.html'

```
#view.py
def d2(request):
    calc=2*2
```

```
        now=datetime.datetime.now()
        t=get_template('date2.html')
        html=t.render(Context({'thedate': now, 'mcalc':calc}))
        return HttpResponse(html)
#urls.py
from fooblah.views import d2
url('^dt/$',d2),
```

Let's modify the root URL and have it point to index.html. Don't forget to create the index.html inside the Django_templates directory. You will also need to import a new library called render_to_response.

```
#views.py
from django.shortcuts import render_to_response
def newroot(request):
    #return HttpResponse("oh wow")
    return render_to_response("index.html")
```

13.1.7. Admin screen

The 'admin' screen is essentially empty because we have not added any models (databases). To pave the way for the management of 'flatpages', add the following to settings.py. In most instances these are default settings already in place.

```
#settings.py
INSTALLED_APPS=(
'django.contrib.admin',
```

Also make sure DATABASE_ENGINE and _NAME is set: ***DATABASE_ENGINE = 'sqlite3'***

DATABASE_NAME = 'whatever.db', now run: ***python manage.py migrate***

It will execute the following lines:

```
Applying contentyptes.0001_initial...OK
Applying auth.0001_initial...OK
...
```

Next you will need to add entries in urls.py, though the default installation might already have this in place.

```
#urls.py
#uncomment admin
from django.contrib import admin
(r'^admin/', include(admin.site.urls)),
```

Now visit the site ***http://127.0.0.1:8000/admin***. You will be prompted with user login screen. There will be two sections called ***Auth*** and **Sites**. ***Auth*** contains Groups and Users. Sites contains Sites which by default is ***example.html***. To make the final connection needed for the project to see the app, add the following to 'settings.py', then create a superuser so you can access the admin screen. Verify you are in the directory containing manage.py or it will not work.

The code to create a superuser is as follows: ***python manage.py createsuperuser***

```
#settings.py
INSTALLED_APPS = (
'django.contrib.flatpages',
'django.contrib.sites',
MIDDLEWARE_CLASSES = (
'django.contrib.flatpages.middleware.FlatpageFallbackMiddleware',
```

Also in settings.py add the following below **ALLOWED_HOSTS =[]**

Please add:

SITES_ID=1

Now run : python manage.py migrate

You will also need to create a directory called 'flatpages' under the 'django_templates' to create a default template. In this case we will use the code below as our template.

```
#default.html
<html>
<body>
{{ flatpage.content }}
</body>
</html>
```

The admin page now contains a flatpage section. Let's add the three flatpages below the the admin screen

/**about**/ page

in the URL: /about/

Title: About whatever

Content: Add the following html

```
<center><h1>About</h1></center>
<p>About our company!!!
<hr>
<p><a href="/about"> about </a>
<p><a href="/info">info</a>
<p><a href="/contact">contact</a>
```

Sites: example.com

/**contact**/ page

Sites: example.com

In the URL: /contact/

Title: Contact

Content: Add the following html

```
<center><h1>Contact</h1></center>
<p>Please contact our engineers at the following number and email
<hr>
<p><a href="/about"> about </a>
<p><a href="/info">info</a>
<p><a href="/contact">contact</a>
```

Sites: example.com

/**info**/ page

Sites: example.com

In the URL: /info/

Title: Information

Content: Add the following html

```
<center><h1>Information</h1></center>
<p>here is my information screen
<hr>
<p><a href="/about"> about </a>
<p><a href="/info">info</a>
<p><a href="/contact">contact</a>
```

Sites: example.com

You can now visit these sites:

```
http://127.0.0.1:8000/about/
http://127.0.0.1:8000/contact/
http://127.0.0.1:8000/info/
```

You can also use base.html as follows:

```
#default.html
{% extends "base.html" %}
```

The base.html is usually found in the templates directory rather than the /flatpages directory. Within base.html you will add ***{{ flatpage.content }}*** in the "block content" statements as follows:

```
{% block content %}
{{ flatpage.content }}
{% endblock %}
```

If you want to use a theme such as getbootstrap.com you can integrate the code into the 'base.html" using popular responsive libraries like bootstrap, boilerplate or grid960.gs. For example, this example uses the carousel theme from getbootstrap.com. The next static content section contains CSS files and/or Javascript files downloaded from getbootstrap.com. You will need to edit the files and change the path for each media file. For example:

```
"/static/dist/js/getbootstrap.min.js"
```

13.1.8. Static Content

All media such as images, videos, Javascript files and CSS style sheets will be placed in the 'static' directory contained within the root directory. You will also need to edit the settings.py as follows

Add these entries to the bottom of the file:

```
STATIC_URL = '/static/'
STATIC_ROOT= 'staticfiles'
```

Add this statement below 'BASE_DIR'

```
STATICFILES_DIRS=(
    os.path.join(BASE_DIR,'static'),
)
```

13.1.9. Basic Blog

Below is the scaffolding of a basic Blog.

```
python manage.py startapp blog

#urls.py
from blog.views import blog
url('^blog/', blog),"

#blog/models.py
class Post(models.Model):
    title=models.CharField(max_length=60)
    body=models.TextField()
    created = models.DateTimeField(auto_now_add=True)
    def __unicode__(self):
        return self.title
```

Also run the following: python manage.py makemigrations
python manage.py migrate

```
#settings.py
add blog to INSTALLED_APPS
```

Now that you have created the model or 'DB' for a blog you can activate the database model by running the following:

python manage.py makemigrations

python manage.py migrate

A copy of the SQL query can be found in the app directory blog/migrations for historical purposes. Within the blog directory, find the admin.py file. If you do not see one, then create a new file and call it admin.py. The admin screen allows you to populate the new blog model you've created.

```
#blog/admin.py
from django.contrib import admin
from blog.models import Post
class PostAdmin(admin.ModelAdmin):
    search_fields=["title"]
admin.site.register(Post,PostAdmin)
```

Now that you have added an 'admin' tag. Visit the website http://localhost:8080/admin. Go to the blog and add a new post! It's just that easy! For the next part, create a couple of dummy posts. This will help us verify that everything is working correctly when we create a view for the new blog content. In the code below, we create a view for the post and 2 new html pages (list.html and base.html).

```
#blog/views.py
from django.core.paginator import Paginator, InvalidPage,
EmptyPage
from django.core.urlresolvers import reverse
from blog.models import *
def blog(request):
    """Main listing."""
    posts = Post.objects.all().order_by("-created")
    paginator = Paginator(posts, 2)
    try: page = int(request.GET.get("page", '1'))
    except ValueError: page = 1
    try:
        posts = paginator.page(page)
    except (InvalidPage, EmptyPage):
        posts = paginator.page(paginator.num_pages)
```

```
return render_to_response("list.html", dict(posts=posts,
user=request.user))

#django_templates/base.html
<head>
<title>
{% block title %}MyBlog{% endblock %}
</title>
</head>
<body>
<div id="sidebar"> {% block sidebar %} {% endblock
%} </div>
<div id="container">
<div id="menu">
{% block nav-global %}
<!- MENU ->
<h3>MyBlog</h3>
{% if user.is_staff %}
<a href="{% url 'admin:index' %}">Admin</a>
<a href="{% url 'admin:blog_post_add %}">Add post</a>
{% endif %}
{% endblock %}
</div>
<div id="content">
{% block content %}{% endblock %}
</div>
</div>
</body>
</html>

#django_templates/list.html
{% extends "base.html" %}
{% block content %}
<div class="main">
<!- Posts ->
<ul>
{% for post in posts.object_list %}
<div class="title">{{ post.title }}</div>
<ul>
<div class="time">{{ post.created }}</div>
<div class="body">{{ post.body|linebreaks }}</div>
</ul>
{% endfor %}
</ul>
<!- Next/Prev page links ->
{% if posts.object_list and posts.paginator.num_pages > 1
%}
<div class="pagination" style="margin-top: 20px; margin-
left: 0px; ">
```

```
<span class="step-links">
{% if posts.has_previous %}
<a href= "#">newer entries &lt;&lt; </a>
{% endif %}
<span class="current">
<p> Page {{ posts.number }} of {{ posts.paginator.num_pages
}}
</span>
{% if posts.has_next %}
<a href="#"> &gt;&gt; older entries</a>
{% endif %}
</span>
</div>|||||||||||||||||||||||||||||||||||||||||||||||||||||||
{% endif %}
</div>
<p><a href="#">Back to Blog Frontpage</a>
{% endblock %}
```

Now run the following: python manage.py migrate and makemigrations. Then visit the site http://localhost:8080/blog

The next section will explain in detail how the Blog works and also how to add comments to each Blog item. The script is useful. I wrote it because I got tired of typing the same methods for each website I would build for a customer. Quickstart your website as follows: ***echo "python manage.py runserver 0.0.0.0:8080" > start.sh***

13.1.10. Blog with Comments

This next section will break the blog down into individual parts and we will insert a comment model for the blog and add some missing elements such as 'author'. This particular site is also using bootstrap CSS static 'navbar' from getbootstrap.com.

Figure 13.1.: blog page

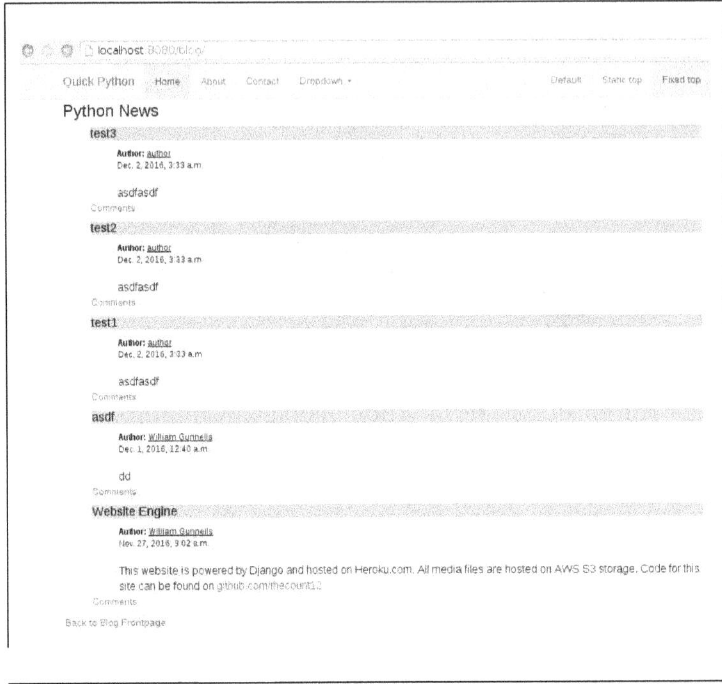

Please adjust the 'urls.py' and add 'blog', 'post' and 'comment' as seen in the example below:

```
#urls.py
from blog.views import post
url('^blog/',blog),
url('^post/(\d+)/$',post),
#url('^comment/(\d+)/$',add_comment),
)
```

The model for creating the database for Blog or news is as follows:

```
#models.py
from django.db import models
class Post(models.Model):
    title=models.CharField(max_length=60)
    body=models.TextField()
```

```
        created = models.DateTimeField(auto_now_add=True)
        author=models.CharField(default='author',max_length=60)
        def __unicode__(self):
            return self.title
```

Also run the following: python manage.py makemigrations
python manage.py migrate

```
#views.py
from django.http import HttpResponseRedirect
def post(request, pk):
    post = Post.objects.get(pk=int(pk))
    comments=Comment.objects.filter(post=post)
    #d = dict(post=post, user=request.user)
    d = dict(post=post, comments=comments,
    form=CommentForm(),user=request.user)
    d.update(csrf(request)) # remove this if csrf not enabled
    return render_to_response("post.html", d)
```

You can add more features to this model such as description tags or an additional date field. This one uses system date upon creation. You can also create post date or simply make it an optional text entry field. Altering a database is pretty simple. Add a new entry such as 'TextField' then run. Because you are altering your model, you now need to run 'sqlmigrate' command below:

```
python manage.py sqlmigrate blog 0002
python manage.py makemigrations
python manage.py migrate
```

The commands above are the list of commands that are run to migrate the model for app. You will need to refresh the server. In the blog directory for that application Django creates an additional directory called /migrations. You can view the history of all the python migration files in that directory for that specific application.

There are a few things to take note of in each of the methods, 'list.html' and 'post.html'. Also notice the commented out code for post by request.user. If they are a registered user on your blog the 'post.html' will allow them access to post an article. But anonymous can post a comment as specified by "d=dict(post=post,comments=comments)". You can easily add "user=request.user" if you want to restrict comments. Also notice 'paginator' and how many posts per page. This example lists '5' posts. The return statements for each method pass the object as a string, list or dictionary. Make adjustments to your list.html as follows.

```
<-!list.html->
{% extends "base.html" %}
{% block content %}
    <div class="main">
        <!- Posts ->
        <ul>
            {% for post in posts.object_list %}
                <div class="title"><h4 style="background-
color: #d3d3d3;">{{ post.title }}</h4></div> <ul>
                <div class="time" style="font-size:smaller;"><b>Author:
</b><u>{{ post.author}}</u></div>
                <div class="time" style="font-size:smaller;">{{
post.created }}</div>
                <div class="body"><br></div>
                <div class="body" style="font-size:medium;">{{
post.body|safe}}</div>
            </ul>
        <div class="commentlink"><a href="/post/{{ post.pk}}">
   Comments</a></div>
            {% endfor %}
        </ul>
        <!- Next/Prev page links ->
        {% if posts.object_list and posts.paginator.num_pages
> 1 %}
        <div class="pagination" style="margin-top: 20px;
margin-left: 0px; ">
            <span class="step-links">
```

```
                {% if posts.has_previous %}
                    <a href= "?page={{ posts.previous_page_number
}}">newer entries &lt;&lt; </a>
                {% endif %}
                <span class="current">
                    <p> Page {{ posts.number }} of
{{ posts.paginator.num_pages }}
                </span>
                {% if posts.has_next %}
                    <a href="?page={{ posts.next_page_number
}}"> &gt;&gt; older entries</a>
                {% endif %}
            </span>
        </div>
        {% endif %}
    </div>
<p><a href="/blog">Back to Blog Frontpage</a>
{% endblock %}
```

My 'blog.html' is a very large HTML file because I'm currently using static 'navbar' from getbootstrap.com. The most import part is the placement of "block content".

```
<!–base.html–>
<ul class="nav navbar-nav navbar-right">
<li><a href="../navbar/">Default</a></li>
<li><a href="../navbar-static-top/">Static top</a></li>
...
...
...
...
...
...
<div id="menu">
{% block nav-global %}
        <h3>Python News</h3>
        {% if user.is_staff %}
        <a href="{% url 'admin:index' %}">Admin</a>
        <a href="{% url 'admin:blog_post_add' %}">Add
post</a>
```

```
        {% endif %}
    {% endblock %}
    </div>
    <div id="content">
    {% block content %}{% endblock %}
    ...
```

The Blog content from 'list.html' loads into this bootstrap page. Also notice the 'nav-global' block statement which loads 'admin' screen if you are a user logged into the system with 'admin' rights.

Main Blog page to load news is 'base.html'. You should have already created this previously. The example below is an adjustment from a modified bootstrap version.

```
<!-base.html->
<head>
<title>
{% block title %}MyBlog{% endblock %}
</title>
</head>
<body>
    <div id="sidebar"> {% block sidebar %} {% end-
block %} </div>
    <div id="container">
        <div id="menu">
            {% block nav-global %}
                <h3>MyBlog</h3>
                {% if user.is_staff %}
                <a href="{% url 'admin:index' %}">Ad-
min</a>
                <a href="{% url 'admin:blog_post_add' %}">Add
post</a>
                {% endif %}
            {% endblock %}
        </div>
        <div id="content">
            {% block content %}{% endblock %}
        </div>
    </div>
```

```
</body> </html>
```

The site can be safely tested without adding the comments method. Add the Comment() model in the example below. You will need to run the following commands after you have added the Comment() model.

```
python manage.py sqlmigrate blog 0002
python manage.py makemigrations
python manage.py migrate
```

It can be helpful to use an appropriate item number 000x which will be different depending on how many changes you have made to the model. Notice the relational element of Comment() model to Post() model. The ForeignKey() is what makes the two tables relational.

```
#models.py
class Comment(models.Model):
    created = models.DateTimeField(auto_now_add=True)
    author = models.CharField(max_length=60)
    body = models.TextField()
    post = models.ForeignKey(Post)

    def __unicode__(self):
        return unicode("%s: %s" % (self.post, self.body[:60]))
```

Also run the following: python manage.py makemigrations
python manage.py migrate

The view will also need to be modified to accommodate the changes for the Comment() model. In views.py, add the following below post() method.

```
from django.forms import ModelForm
from django.core.context_processors import csrf
class CommentForm(ModelForm):
    class Meta:
        model = Comment
        exclude = ["post"]
```

Below CommentForm() add add_comment() model to views.py:

```
def add_comment(request, pk):
    p = request.POST
    if p.has_key("body") and p["body"]:
        author = "Anonymous"
        if p["author"]: author = p["author"]
        comment = Comment(post=Post.objects.get(pk=pk))
        cf = CommentForm(p, instance=comment)
        cf.fields["author"].required = False
        comment = cf.save(commit=False)
        comment.author = author
        comment.save()
    #return HttpResponseRedirect(reverse("blog.views.post",
args=[pk]))
    #return render_to_response('list.html',pk)
```

Next is 'post.html'. This page will display the post contents and if comments exist will also display those comments as well as allow you to submit a new comment.

```
<!-post.html->
{% extends "base.html" %}
{% block content %}
<div class="title"><h4>{{ post.title }}</h4></div>
<ul>
    <div class="time"><b>Author: </b><u>{{ post.author}}</u>
    <div class="time">{{ post.created }}</div>
    <div class="body">{{ post.body|safe}}</div>
</ul>

{% if comments %}
    <p>Comments:</p>
{% endif %}
{% for comment in comments %}
    <div class="comment">
        <div class="time">{{ comment.created }} | {{
comment.author }}</div>
        <div class="body">{{ comment.body|linebreaks }}</div>
    </div>
{% endfor %}
```

```
<br> <hr>
<div id="addc">Add a comment</div>
<!- Comment form ->
<form action="/comment/{{post.pk}}/" method="POST">
  <div id="cform">
    Name: {{ form.author }}
    <p>{{ form.body|linebreaks }}</p>
  </div>
  <div id="submit"><input type="submit" value="Submit"></div>
</form>
{% endblock %}

#urls.py
from blog.view import add_comment
url('^comment/(\d+)/$',blog.views.add_comment),
```

You now have a complete Blog system with the ability to add comments and other additional features as well as an 'admin' tool that you didn't need to configure.

13.1.11. Registration

Here is a quick example of how to create a registration model, form, and view. You can utilize this example to create any other form you want or even a poll.

Run the following command: *python manage.py startapp reg*

Please don't forget to change to the correct directory and edit the following files in the reg directory.

```
#models.py
class REG(models.Model):
  username=models.CharField(max_length=100)
  email=models.CharField(max_length=100)
  password=models.CharField(max_length=100)
  hint=models.CharField(max_length=100)
  date=models.DateField()
  def __unicode__(self):
```

```
        return """Username: %s saved,
            please wait for approval""" % (self.username)
```

Edit settings.py and add reg to the INSTALLED_APPS 'reg',

Also run the following: python manage.py makemigrations
python manage.py migrate

```
#forms.py
# you might need to create this if it doesn't
#exist in the reg directory
from django import forms
from models import REG
class PostReg(forms.ModelForm):
    class Meta:
        model=REG
        fields=('username','email','password','hint',)

#admin.py
from django.contrib import admin
from models import REG
class RegAdmin(admin.ModelAdmin):
    display_fields=["username","email"]
    search_fields=["username"]
    list_display=["username","email"]
admin.site.register(REG,RegAdmin)

#views.py
from django.shortcuts import render
from forms import PostReg
from django.shortcuts import render_to_response
def newreg(request):
    # use next two lines to view form first before testing
if statement
    # form=PostReg()
    # return render(request,'reg.html', {'form':form})
    if request.method == "POST":
        form = PostReg(request.POST)
        if form.is_valid():
```

```
            post = form.save(commit=False)
            #post.author = request.user
            post.date= "2015-05-18"
            #use python date libs
            post.save()
        #return redirect('blog.views.post_detail', pk=post.pk)
        return render_to_response("thanks.html")
    else:
        form = PostReg()
    return render(request, 'reg.html', {'form': form})
```

```
#urls.py
from reg.views import reg
url('^reg/', newreg),

#django_templates/reg.html
{% extends "base.html" %}
{% block content %}
<h1>New post</h1>
<form method="POST" class="post-form">{% csrf_token
%}
  {{ form.as_p }}
<button type="submit" class="save btn btn-default">Save</button>
</form>
{% endblock %}

#django_templates/thanks.html
{% extends "base.html" %}
{% block content %}
<h1>Thanks for registering</h1>
{% endblock %}
```

13.1.12. CBV vs FBV

There is much discussion about 'class based views' vs. 'function based views'. Though function based views are easier to write, the trend leans more toward 'class based views'. You may start writing function based views at the beginning of a new project and then transition to class based views later.

CBV is abstracted code with a smaller footprint and some argue that it's more reusable. The example below will demonstrate a user signup form that also extends the core User built into Django. If you are interested in knowing more, read about the experiences of other developers on your favorite forums like reddit.

```
#root urls.py
import signup.views
    url(r'^signup/',signup.views.Signup),

#models.py
from django.contrib.auth.models import User
from django.db.models.signals import post_save
from django.dispatch import receiver
class Profile(models.Model):
    user = models.OneToOneField(User, on_delete=models.CASCADE)
    fullnameandaddress = models.TextField(max_length=500,
blank=True)
    location = models.CharField(max_length=30, blank=True)
    birthdate = models.DateField(null=True, blank=True)
@receiver(post_save, sender=User)
def update_user_profile(sender, instance, created, **kwargs):
    if created:
        Profile.objects.create(user=instance)
    instance.profile.save()
```

After you create the model please run the following command:

```
python manage.py makemigrations

python manage.py migrate
```

```
#forms.py
from django import forms
from django.contrib.auth.forms import UserCreationForm
from django.contrib.auth.models import User
class SignUpForm(UserCreationForm):
    birthdate = forms.DateField(help_text='Required. Format: YYYY-MM-DD')
    class Meta:
        model = User
```

```
        fields = ('username', 'birthdate', 'password1', 'pass-
word2', )

    #views.py
    from django.contrib.auth import login, authenticate
    from django.shortcuts import render, redirect
    from signup.forms import SignUpForm
    def Signup(request):
        if request.method == 'POST':
            form = SignUpForm(request.POST)
            if form.is_valid():
                user = form.save()
                user.refresh_from_db() # load the profile
                user.profile.birthdate = form.cleaned_data.get('birth_date')
                user.save()
                raw_password = form.cleaned_data.get('password1')
                user = authenticate(username=user.username,
password=raw_password)
                login(request, user) return redirect('/')
        else:
            form = SignUpForm()
        return render(request, 'signup.html', {'form': form})

    <!- signup.html ->
    {% extends 'base.html' %}
    {% block content %}
    <h2>Sign up</h2>
    <form method="post">
    {% csrf_token %}
    {{ form.as_p }}
    <button type="submit">Sign up</button>
    </form>
    {% endblock %}

    #admin.py
    from signup.models import Profile
    from django.contrib.auth.admin import UserAdmin
    from django.contrib.auth.models import User
    class ProfInline(admin.StackedInline):
        model=Profile
    class ProfAdmin(admin.ModelAdmin):
```

```
    inlines = (ProfInline,)
admin.site.unregister(User)
admin.site.register(User,ProfAdmin)
```

The example above is a very simplified way to add a model, form and view which extend the User library by adding a profile model. The admin.py will utilize the 'inline' method which will combine the model within the Users admin screen.

Visit your site: http://localhost:8000/admin

Select users. 'Profile' model will now be visible with addition data for that user.

13.1.13. exercises

1. Get the blog working.
2. Style adjustments to templates.
3. Get flatpages working on blog site.
4. Add blog content through the admin interface.
5. Add comment method and your own custom features
6. Combine Bootstrap and Django. You can leverage the built-in library for bootstrap tools.

- python-bootstrapform - generate twitter-bootstrap form output for django form - Python 2.x
- python-bootstrapform-doc - generate twitter-bootstrap form output for django form - doc
- python3-bootstrapform - generate twitter-bootstrap form output for django form - Python 3.x
- pip install django-boostrap3 - make template into bootstrap 3 code

14. Apache, Heroku, AWS and Cloud

14.1. Additional Django Features

Apache

It's pretty easy to add Django to a platform that supports Apache Web Server. The example below is a configuration for a website called thinktank.com. You can skip this section if you don't have Apache installed. Replace thinktank with the name of your Django site. Please notice you are creating an alias to a full path.

```
Alias /media/ /home/knoppix/thinktank/media/
Alias /static/ /home/knoppix/thinktank/static/
```

Edit and Adjust the file 'httpd.conf' or 'site-enabled' directory and whatever your sites 'name_configuration.conf'.

```
WSGIScriptAlias / /home/knoppix/thinktank/thinktank/wsgi.py/
<Directory /home/knoppix/thinktank>
<Files wsgi.py>
Allow from all
Order allow,deny
</Files>
</Directory>
```

Contained within 'wsgi.py':

```
import os
from django.core.wsgi import get_wsgi_application
os.environ.setdefault("DJANGO_SETTINGS_MODULE",
"thinktank.settings")
application = get_wsgi_application()
```

Below is a more complete example:

```
NameVirtualHost *:80
<VirtualHost *:80>
  ServerAdmin webmaster@localhost
  ServerName thinktank.com
  ServerAlias www.thinktank.com
  #DocumentRoot /var/www/thinktank
  <Directory />
    Options FollowSymLinks
    AllowOverride None
  </Directory>
  <Directory /var/www/>
    Options Indexes FollowSymLinks MultiViews
    AllowOverride None
    Order allow,deny
    allow from all
  </Directory>
  WSGIScriptAlias / /var/www/thinktank/thinktank/wsgi.py/
  Alias /static /var/www/thinktank/static/
  WSGIDaemonProcess sfoobar user=webdj group=webdj
processes=2 threads=24
  WSGIProcessGroup sfoobar
```

14.1.1. Heroku

Publishing to Heroku is also pretty simple. First go to heroku.com and register a new account and read the basic documentation. After you have gone through the basic documentation come back to this section and perform the following steps:

Table 14.1.: Install the required packages

pip install dj-datbase-url
pip install dj-static
pip install static3
pip install gunicorn

1. Create a django site locally in linux. Design and test it.

   a) Create Procfile and add the following (please take note of the double hyphen and single hyphen at the end. The procfile tells heroku which process to start in order to sever the project properly. It is a one-line file that should be saved as Procfile and no extension): *web: gunicorn sitename.wsgi –log-file -*

   b) Create requirements.txt and add the following items to the file. Don't enumerate the file.

      Django==1.10 #or greater
      dj-database-url==0.3.0 # you will be using heroku PostgressSQL
      dj-static==0.0.6 # heroku static directory this is ephemeral
      django-toolbelt==0.0.1
      gunicorn==19.7.0
      pysycopg2==2.5.3
      static3==0.5.1
      wsgiref==0.1.2

      i. some of my other sites use the following django-storages==1.4.1, boto==2.34.0 and awscli==1.10.47 so I can store stuff on Amazon S3 storage. The requirements sometimes can be a little tricky to create. In some cases I will create an additional requirements file by using "pip freeze > stable-req.txt". This will generate a list of all installed library versions on my current system. However I won't use all the libraries that I want published to Heroku, but I will be able to extract the correct version number for the library I want to utilize. Requirements file will also take additional symbols such as '>' or '*' for additional range of versions.

2. Please note some of the above values may change. For instance (Django==1.8.7 was the current version I was using when I started this chapter. Gunicorn also changes I was running version 19.0.0)

3. Login or Register for a free heroku site

4. Download and install the heroku toolbelt

5. *heroku login*

6. Create new git

7. Change to the django site directory such as 'blah' or whatever you named your django site.
8. Run the command in that directory and the command below: *git init*
9. *heroku git: remote -a heroku_ sitename_ you_ registered*
10. Deploy application with the following commands below. Please note you will run the 3 commands below multiple times when you are deploying multiple versions or changes to your website.
11. *git add .*
12. *git commit -am "first upload"*
13. *git push heroku master*

The site should be running locally and tested, but then you will need to connect to heroku and run it for the first time. At that point, the two commands below will be run multiple times:

heroku run python manage.py makemigrate
heroku run python manage.py migrate

Run "heroku open". Steps 7 through 12 will be repeated as you refine your site.

You will also need to comment out the DATABASES section in settings and use 'djtools' as follows:

DATABASES={'default':dj_ database_ url.config()}

Also import the following in 'settings.py': ***import dj_ database_ url.***

The rest of the configuration is making sure that you have static media setup correctly. Remember that the storage is ephemeral. What this means is that you can push your files to the server as static files. Media files added later will be deleted. I recall that I had to run python manage.py collectstatic on heroku server a few times to explicitly keep my media from becoming purged. I recommend using AWS S3 storage to maintain your media files.

14.1.2. Amazon AWS S3 storage

You will need to create an account on amazon AWS and read the basic documentation for S3 storage. You get to utilize a storage system called 'S3' free for a year.

Here is an example of amazon s3 storage. You will be adding this to the bottom of your 'settings.py'.

```
AWS_STORAGE_BUCKET_NAME = 'bucket_name_site_name'
AWS_QUERYSTRING_AUTH=False
AWS_ACCESS_KEY_ID = 'access_key'
AWS_SECRET_ACCESS_KEY = 'secret_access_key'
AWS_S3_CUSTOM_DOMAIN = '%s.s3-website-us-west-
2.amazonaws.com' % AWS_STORAGE_BUCKET_NAME
STATIC_URL = '/static/'
STATIC_ROOT='staticfiles'
MEDIA_ROOT='media'
MEDIAFILES_LOCATION='media'
MEDIA_URL='https://%s/' % AWS_S3_CUSTOM_DOMAIN
DEFAULT_FILE_STORAGE = "storages.backends.s3boto.
S3BotoStorage"
```

On aws.amazon.com inside the s3 Mangement Console, I created a bucket called 'bucket_name_site_name'. The bucket also has permissions. I granted my users full access to 'Everyone' with list and view access, however there is an Edit bucket policy.

```
{
"Version": "2008-10-17",
"Statement":[
{
"Sid":"AllowPublicRead",
"Effect":"Allow",
"Principal":{
"AWS":"*"
},
"Action":"S3:GetObject",
"Resource":"Arn:Aws:S3:::Mvda194s3/*"
}
}
}
```

The configuration settings above are very weak with regards to security. This configuration is recommended for simple storage of images, audio files, and documents. If more security is needed, run the git commands above, then run "collectstatic". Notice that no changes were made to "CORS". Keep in mind that you have limited storage on heroku. This is why I recommend learning to use AWS services.

Admin

The django-admin is crazy powerful as you might have discovered playing around. You can can easily create a site, build a model, and import data. An admin can begin data manipulation within minutes of creating the site using only the admin screen. You can also make easy adjustments to admin such as list_display=[] and search_fields=[], and pass the table values as a list of what you want to display or search

Generic Generic Views

Here is an extremely fast method of creating a db model, and a view to display your new data:

add to models.py

```
class Officer(models.Model):
    Officer=models.CharField(max_length=60)
    Name=models.CharField(max_length=60)
    Phone=models.CharField(max_length=60)
    email=models.CharField(max_length=60)
    upjewel=models.FileField(upload_to="images/")
    def __unicode__(self):
        return self.Officer
```

Also run the following: python manage.py makemigrations
python manage.py migrate

add to views.py

```
from django.views.generic import ListView
```

```
class listofficer(ListView):
    model=Officer
```

Depending on which model you put this under, it will look for that file in that directory example:

The location of my file was found in:

django_templates/blog/officer_list.html.

You can check the log files for this and add the following to officer_list.html. This example uses the 'getbootstrap' jumbo theme

```
{% extends "blogbase.html" %}
{% block content %}
<H3>Officers Of 2018</H3>
<ul>
{% for B In object_list %}
    <li style="list-style:none;">
    <Img Src="../../media/{{B.upjewel}}" height="70"
width="70" style="float:left;margin: 0 10px 0 0">
    {{B.Officer}}: {{B.Name}}
    <Br>{{B.Phone}}
    <Br>{{B.Email}}
    <Br> <Br> <Br>
    </li>
{% endfor %}
</ul>
{% endblock %}
```

Please notice the in-line CSS. This is not recommended best practice but I wanted to illustrate how simple it is to dress up the page and iterate the contents of the model() using object_list built in function for extracting objects from the model you created. Add the following to urls.py

```
url('^officers/',listofficer.as_view()),


#admin.py
from blog.models import Officer
class OfficerAdmin(admin.ModelAdmin):
    display_fields=["officer"]
admin.site.register(Officer,OfficerAdmin)
```

This model uses 'FileField' to upload images. You will also need to adjust 'urlpatterns' in 'url.py' to include the ability to add media files.

```
#urls.py
from django.conf import settings
from django.conf urls.static import static
urlpatterns = [
    url('^officers/',listofficer.as_view()),
] + static(settings.MEDIA_URL,
document_root=settings.MEDIA_ROOT)
```

Your 'urlspatterns' field might be very large so the only change you need to make is to append the +static().

You also need to edit 'settings.py' and add the following to the end of the file.

```
MEDIA_ROOT='media'
MEDIA_URL='/media'/
```

Create a directory called 'media/images' in the root of your 'django' project to store your image files.

Test first locally then 'git push' and test remotely. If you are not using AWS, the files will only be stored temporarily because Heroku's file system is ephemeral. The example above shows the admin screen with the ability to upload files.

REST Representation State Transfer

There are already many tools for REST API. Django has a Rest Framework API library or you can use the popular TastyPie library. Either way Django is inherently designed to be RESTful. These are the RESTful URL design tags to add , append, edit and delete objects in a RESTFul application.

```
http://localhost:8080/blog
http://localhost:8080/blog/add
http://localhost:8080/blog/1
http://localhost:8080/blog/1/edit
http://localhost:8080/blog/1/delete
```

This simple design is not always easy to do correctly. Even with a proven framework such as the Rest Framework API or

TastyPie, the only thing missing from the above example is lsimplejsonl and some serialization or XML. Shown below are two examples illustrating how to utilize 'simplejson'.

```
from django.http import JsonResponse
def blahview(request):
    data={}
    return JsonResponse(data)
#and or serialize
    #html=render_to_string("blah.html", data)
    #serial_data=simplejson.dumps({"html":html})
    #return HttpResponse(serial_data,mimetype="application/json:)
```

So if you are in a bind, you can whip up your own implementation of REST or utilize a proper library (highly recommended).

15. UML

15.1. UML

Unified Modeling Language (UML) is a modeling language used in object-oriented software engineering. The standard was created by Object Management Group (OMG) a consortium that sets standards for distributed object-oriented systems and modeling programs and processes for model-based standards. UML has a visual set of models that construct and document artifacts of an object-oriented software development system. There are nine modeling diagrams that represent the architectural blueprints of the systems development environment.

- Use case diagrams
- Class diagrams
- Object diagrams
- Sequence diagrams
- Collaboration diagrams
- Statechart diagrams
- Activity diagrams
- Component diagrams
- Deployment diagrams

15.1.1. Use Case diagrams

Use-case diagrams describe applications from the position of the external observer. It contains a stick figure for an actor, a message arrow to represent communication, and an oval to represent use-case.

Figure 15.1.: Use Case

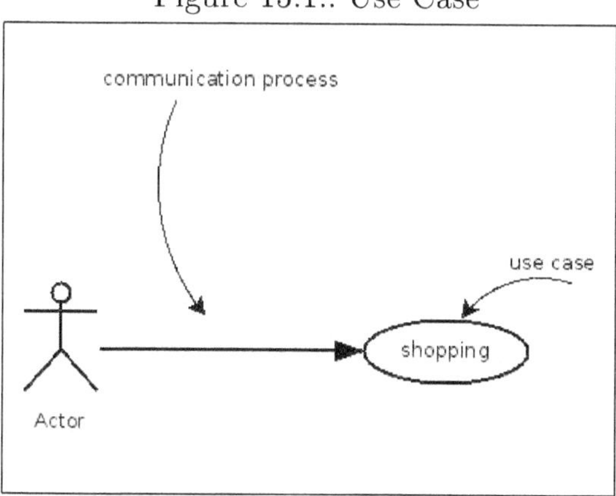

You can have a single actor initiate multiple message requests to a single use case or several use case processes. The benefits of these types of diagrams are to demonstrate scenarios for application features.

15.1.2. Class diagrams

The class diagram gives an overview of the systems relationship with another static class relationships. The class relationship consists of the following:

- association - a relationship between two or more classes designated by a line connecting the class diagrams.
- aggregation - an association represented by a diamond connecting to the end as part containing the whole
- generalization - is a link represented by a triangle designating a superclass.
- multiplicity - represented by (0..1) zero or 1 instance, (0..*) no limit, 1 exactly 1 instance,or (1..*) at least one instance.

Every diagram should have at least a class, association, and multiplicities.

Figure 15.2.: Class Diagram

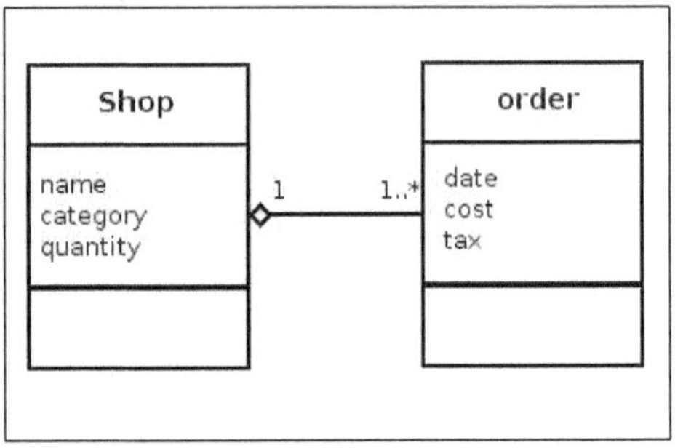

15.1.3. Object diagrams

Class diagrams can be exceptionally detailed and utilize a lot of space. From a visual perspective, they may seem to clutter up the screen though they can be very helpful. An object diagram is a condensed diagram listing only the classes and their dependencies.

Figure 15.3.: Object Diagrams

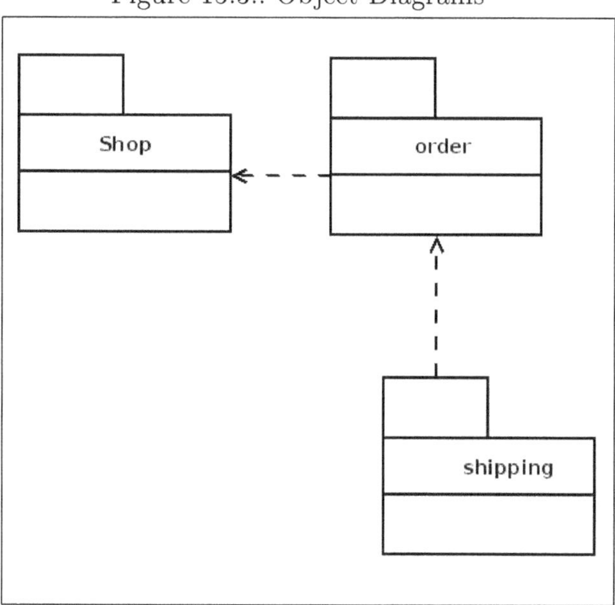

15.1.4. Activity diagrams

Sequence diagrams, collaboration diagrams, and 'statechart' diagrams, are well beyond the scope of this chapter. Activity diagrams are similar to flowcharts that show how activities depend on one another. The activity chart uses the same symbols as the state chart with the exception of the state bubble. The state chart focuses on the flow of the process transitions rather than the overall flow. The widgets of an activity include the following:

1. Start and stop - designated as dark dot
2. Activity - square with rounded edges. More rounded then state widget.
3. Transition - line with arrows connecting activities and branches.

4. Branch - represented by a diamond do indicate a decision.
5. Fork/union - represented by short thick bold line.

Figure 15.4.: Activity Diagram

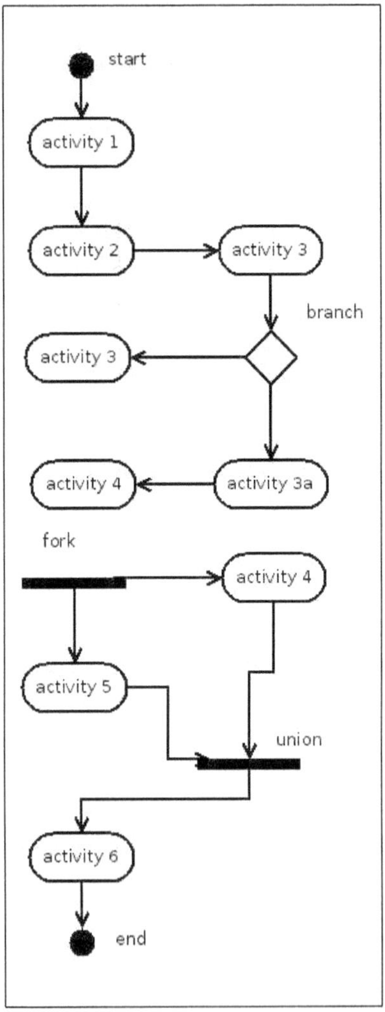

Component diagrams and deployment diagrams are well beyond the scope of this book and chapter.

15.1.5. Dia and UML

Dia is a GTK+ based diagram creation program used in Linux or Windows. It's similar to Visio but very light weight. The benefits are the ability to extend the programs widgets and design capabilities with XML. You can download dia at http://dia-installer.de/. For Mac users it's possible you will also need to install XQuarts. For our purposes 'DIA' contains a special object to draw UML diagrams. Dia also contains a plug-in for python scripting and includes several python scripts to extend, convert, manipulate 'dia' or code resulting from or related to 'dia'. Below is the tool bar and canvas screen:

Figure 15.5.: DIA

Let's play with DIA. Select the class widget from the UML widget screen. Click anywhere on the screen. The result should look as follows:

Figure 15.6.: DIA class widget

The next step is to right click on the widget (or double click for Mac users) and select properties. To delete an object, you can click the object and type (CTRL-X). You should have five tabs at the top of the screen labeled Class, Attributes, Operations, Templates, and Style. Click the 'Class' tab and rename the file Shop. Next, select Attributes. Create 4 attributes by selecting "New" and entering the attributes name in the "Name:" field with the following list items: fruits, meats, dairy, and juice. Your screen should look as follows:

Figure 15.7.: DIA UML Properties

Now select the Operations tab. Create two operations. The first will be an "__init__". Make sure visibility is Private and the Parameters are fruits, meats, dairy, and juice. Create another operation called 'myprint' with Visibility set to Public. Your screen should look as follows:

Figure 15.8.: DIA UML Operations

Now save the file as classshop.dia. The next step is to convert the code as follows:

dia2code -t python classshop.dia.

It will create a file called Shop.py in the same directory where Dia was executed. The file is named after the Class field name on the first tab.

```
class Shop:
    """Class Shop
    """
# Attributes:
fruits = None # ()
meats = None # ()
dairy = None # ()
juice = None # ()
```

```
    # Operations
    def myprint(self):
        """function myprint
        returns
        """
        return None # should raise NotImplementedEr-
ror()
    def ____init__(self, fruits, meats, dairy, juice):
        """function __init__
        fruits:
        meats:
        dairy:
        juice:
        returns
        """
        return None # should raise NotImplementedEr-
ror()
```

As you can see, it leaves you with the class structure. All it needs now is to be re-factored. Remove the comments except for attributes as they are a sample placeholders for your future code. Don't forget to remove the extra underscore characters in ____init__ to be __init__. I usually swap the constructor with 'myprint' statement. Here is the re-factored code:

```
class Shop:
    """Class Shop
"""
    fruits = None # ()
    meats = None # ()
    dairy = None # ()
    juice = None # ()
    def __init__(self, fruits, meats, dairy, juice):
        self.fruits=fruits
        self.meats=meats
        self.dairy=dairy
        self.juice=juice
```

```
    def myprint(self):
        print "fruit= ", self.fruits
myclass=Shop("apple","steak","eggs","berry")
myclass.myprint()
```

The program dia2code is by no means perfect. There are tons of other UML editors out there but this one is open source and works with python. The idea is to rapidly prototype something using a visual tool then export it to functional code. There are other UML tools that are more robust but they have weaknesses as well. Cost being the primary weakness. The other is language compatibility. With dia you have a great deal of flexibility. You can sit in a meeting and immediately start flow charting and modeling an application as it is being discussed.

The visual aspects of the code become immensely important for marketing purposes and for managers that have no programming experience. Since documentation is sparse on the web, you can reverse engineer more of "dia uml" details and configuration using "dia2uml" or "autodia". 'Autodia' will create an xml file as follows:

```
autodia -l python -i Shop.py -o newname.xml
```

You can then open the file: dia newname.xml

You may receive errors such as "Taking string value of non-string node". These errors occur when you start initializing the Class and or variables. This is enough information to rapidly prototype an application, and have a visual representation of the code for marketing purposes.

15.1.6. Exercises

1. Optimize the existing code.

16. Game Programming

16.1. Game Programming

Have you ever wondered how hard it would be to create a computer game? Now that you have some practice writing python, you might wonder if python is good enough for building games. The answer would be an excited "Oh Yes". Though you will need to do patiently plan, design and then write the actual code your game, testing as you code. The bottom line is that it can be done. You probably want to start with a formal GDD (game design document), which is a full description of the game in detail and often exceeds 30 pages. It's very similar to a book proposal but with more technical detail.

Everyone should write a game engine at least once to fully appreciate the insanity that's involved with commercial engines such as Unreal, Unity, Blender and more. When it comes to programming nearly anything, it is ideal to write code that's reusable. Methods that draw images or play sounds can be reused on every game project you decide to create. Before designing a game engine you must take into consideration essential requirements and basic limitations. Everything should be mapped out in a tool such as UML on what the engine specifically targets. For instance a 2D engine will lack 3D drawing capabilities while 3D can draw amazing graphics but have slower 2D drawing procedures. The engine should be simple but effective and have a modular design. The modules should be broken down into 4 main sections: graphics, audio, input and message passing.

It would also be good to remember that the original game idea you have in mind will evolve. No matter how clever you are or how graphically skilled you are, expect that more than 80% of your ideas will change and sometimes dramatically . This classic 80/20 rule of thumb is informed from talking to many very experienced game developers.

16.1.1. Where to begin?

There is plenty of code out there that is written for beginners. If you have to start from scratch, there will be many problems. The experts reuse the same methods over and over; methods such as import, initialize, screen, construct images, load, main loop, and more. Often the trade secrets are in graphics acceleration and algorithms.

16.1.2. Above all!

It is smart to avoid designing in another person's game engine. The engine was built specifically for their game development environment and their idea or perspective. While using their game engine, you will be restricted to their ideas. This can feel frustrating if you are new to game development. They could also decide that they want to sell their engine with all the bells and whistles as a commercial product. You can do this too! It is important to become very proficient at re-using code. Should you play with game engines? Absolutely. In fact it is mandatory to explore and find those limitations. The act of playing with the game engine will give you plenty of ideas. Blender is an example of a 3D Graphics Modeling tool that can be modified into a 3D game engine environment. It can be helpful to prototype a new game idea using an existing game engine.

16.1.3. Graphics

Some of the best and most addictive games have mediocre graphics, but they have quality game play. Graphics can always improve later as you move forward with your idea.

16.1.4. Minimum requirements for a Game Programmer

1. **Introduction to programming** - We have covered some of these topics already. But more importantly you need to understand how to solve problems.
2. **Programming Languages** - Learning C and C++ would be a great stepping stone toward mastery of game programming. What you develop in python you can easily convert to C/C++. Start with stripping away the libraries. However if you leverage popular graphics libraries such as SDL and OpenGL the changes are few and subtle. You will spend more time dealing with parsers and analyzers.
3. **Data Structures and & Algorithms** - This is by far the most important topic for programming anything at any level. Testing and mastering arrays, linked lists, binary trees, general trees, hash tables, and heaps will get you a job anywhere. Most people learn them and forget them, then barely get hired as a developer and many change careers.
4. **Compilers** - Let's face it, if you need it to be faster you need to understand concepts such as tokenizing, parsing, code generation, and garbage collection.
5. **Operating Systems** - You need to know the limitations of your OS. Knowledge of threading, locking, network communication, and device drivers is invaluable for multi-player games or reading bits of a DVD-ROM and displaying graphics from a 3D card.
6. **Artificial Intelligence** - Heuristics, planning, algorithms, bayesian networks and natural language parsing add reality concepts to your gaming environment.
7. **Databases** - You have to keep this data somewhere.

16.1.5. Game Theory

How do you make something that others want to play? This can be a daunting task. Game companies and marketing analysts research latest trends to gather this information. There is a fine balance between themes, map design, level features, sound, story, and game play difficulty. In the end you want your game to look good and be fun to play. This means you must take a balanced approach during as you move from concept to deployment.

16.1.6. Prototype

In reality your dream and ideas won't come to fruition until you actually start writing code. You will start building your first prototype and then another until you have several prototype versions. Much can be learned from a prototype such as the general concept and how to play. You also discover more realities such as menus, screen transitions, and how to save or load a game. Here are a few things to think about:

1. Do you need a story teller?
2. Do you need an algorithm expert?
3. Do you need a graphic artist? Raster, Vector or both.
4. Do you need a musician or sound technician?

A prototype can also quickly tell you if the game is worth it or not.

Things to study:

1. Best path, shortest path. Dijkstra's Bellman-Ford
2. Collision Detection/Avoidance Behaviors
3. Projectile Motion and Vectors
4. Map Generation, Tile Generation
5. Grid Design Pixel, Coordination System.

Figure 16.1.: zero-sum

		Odd	
		head	tail
Even	head	1,-1	-1,1
	tail	-1,1	1,-1

6. Algorithms -

   a. Minimax - is a decision rule for minimizing the possible loss while maximizing the potential gain. This can also be thought of as 'maximizing the minimum gain'.

Minimax Theorem according to Wikipedia.org established by John Von Neumann states:

> For every two-person, zero-sum game with finite strategies, there exists a
> value V and a mixed strategy for each player, such that (a) Given player
> 2's strategy, the best payoff possible for player 1 is V, and (b)
> Given players 1's strategy, the best payoff possible for player 2 is - V.

16.1.7. Zero-sum

If we add the wins and losses in a game, treating losses as negatives, we find that the sum is zero for each set of strategies chosen, then the game is a zero-sum game. If a strategy set for which the sum differs from zero, then the game is not zero sum. An example would be a single coin toss.

16.2. Pygame

Pygame is a cross-platform set of modules for writing games. Pygame is the replacement for the Simple Direct Media Layer (SDL) Library. The goal was to allow real-time computer game development without the need for exhaustive low-level C programming to drive the graphical elements of game development. This allows game developers to focus more on game logic rather than level programming. Go to pygame.org and download pygame or run *'pip install pygame'* from the terminal.

The basic concepts for creating a game are user input, output and basic world simulation. The tools to do this are as follows:

1. Input/Output handling - keyboard, mouse, and joystick.
2. Screen display - shapes, drawing, image blitting, and font rendering
3. Sound - effects and music
4. help('pygame')

16.2.1. Screen Initialization

Before starting with screen initialization let's take note that the pygame.init() is actually a tuple.

```
import pygame
x=pygame.init()
print x
```

Results: (6,0)

```
import pygame
pygame.init()
while 1: # this loop function will keep the display up.
    screen = pygame.display.set_mode((1024,768))
```

Results: a blank screen pop up

```
#display1.py
import pygame
pygame.init()
mydisplay=pygame.display.set_mode((800,600))
print pygame.display.set_mode((800,600))
mode=help('pygame.display.set_mode')
display=help('pygame.display')
print mode
print display
```

Results: enter 'q' multiple times to cycle through help in display_set_mode and all of pygame display functions.

16.2.2. Event Handling

The core events in pygame are as follows:

Table 16.1.: Events

Event	Description
QUIT	none
ACTIVEEVENT	gain,state
KEYDOWN	unicode,key,mod
KEYUP	key,mod
MOUSEMOTION	pos,rel,buttons
MOUSEBUTTON	pos,button
MOUSEBUTTONDOWN	pos,button
VIDEORESIZE	size,w,h
VIDEOEXPOSE	none
USEREVENT	code

Here is a practical example of moving a rectangle across the screen. Ctrl-C to exit

```
#pygameEvent1.py
import pygame
white=(255,255,255) # RGB values
```

```
black=(0,0,0)
pygame.init()
display=pygame.display.set_mode((800,600))
x=300; y=300
while 1:
  for event in pygame.event.get(): # event handling
    if event.type==pygame.KEYDOWN:
      if event.key == pygame.K_LEFT:
        x -= 10
      if event.key == pygame.K_RIGHT:
        x += 10
  display.fill(white) # not rendered yet without update
  pygame.draw.rect(display,black,[x,y,10,10]) # w,h
  pygame.display.update() # always update after graph-
ics
 pygame.quit()
 quit()
```

Figure 16.2.: pygame window

Results: You can move your rectangle keys left and right. If you duplicated the steps for 'y', the new rectangle will move in all directions. Now we implement 'xChange' and 'yChange' to prevent values of 'x' and 'y' from going beyond the borders. Before we test this, let's first make a few adjustments for continuous motion. The example below will go beyond the borders.

Example: This allows you to move the rectangle in any direction. The position of (x,y) correspond to Cartesian coordinate system starting in the top left corner of your monitor.

```
#pygameEvent2.py
import pygame
white=(255,255,255) # RGB values
black=(0,0,0)
pygame.init()
display=pygame.display.set_mode((800,600))
x=300; y=300
xChange=0; yChange=0
clock = pygame.time.Clock()
while 1:
  for event in pygame.event.get(): # event handling
    if event.type==pygame.KEYDOWN:
      if event.key == pygame.K_LEFT:
        xChange = - 10
        yChange = 0 # comment out for diagonal
      elif event.key == pygame.K_RIGHT:
        xChange = 10
        yChange = 0
      elif event.key == pygame.K_UP:
        yChange = - 10
        xChange = 0
      elif event.key == pygame.K_DOWN:
        yChange = 10
        xChange = 0
  x += xChange
  y += yChange
  display.fill(white) # not rendered without update
  pygame.draw.rect(display,black,[x,y,10,10]) #w,h
  pygame.display.update()
  clock.tick(10)
pygame.quit()
quit()
```

The clock becomes important when an event occurs automatically and defaults to your system clock. First person shooter games usually have a clock tick of 15 frames per second (FPS)while video clips are round 24-30 (FPS). Make sure the update is in the main loop and that it's near the end. In this case, I put clock tick after display.update(). This is also important when changing event rates. Sometimes it's better to change (x,y) values rather than adjust tick().

16.2.3. Borders

Continuing from the previous example, an 'if' statement is commented out that breaks the border loop. If you uncomment this statement, and comment out the next 'if/elif' statement, the game loop will break.

```
#pygameEvent3.py
import pygame
white=(255,255,255) # RGB values
black=(0,0,0)
pygame.init()
display=pygame.display.set_mode((800,600))
x=300; y=300
xChange=0; yChange=0
clock = pygame.time.Clock()
while 1:
  for event in pygame.event.get(): # event handling
    if event.type==pygame.KEYDOWN:
      if event.key == pygame.K_LEFT:
        xChange = - 10
        yChange = 0
      elif event.key == pygame.K_RIGHT:
        xChange = 10
        yChange = 0
      elif event.key == pygame.K_UP:
        yChange = - 10
        xChange = 0
      elif event.key == pygame.K_DOWN:
```

```
                yChange = 10
                xChange = 0
        # if x >= 800 or x <= 0 or y >= 600 or y <= 0:
# border
            # break
        if x == 700:
            xChange=-10
            yChange=0
        elif x==10:
            xChange=0
            yChange=0
        x += xChange
        y += yChange
        display.fill(white) # not rendered without update
        pygame.draw.rect(display,black,[x,y,10,10]) # coords,
w,h
        pygame.display.update()
        clock.tick(10)
    pygame.quit()
    quit()
```

Results: When the rectangle scrolls to the right and reaches position '700', it will bounce in the opposite direction. However, when the rectangle reaches position '10', it stops everything. This is a great example of a logic problem. Adjust the value of 'xChange=0' to '10' in the 'elif' statement and now the rectangle bounces back and forth across the screen as continues moving while the keys are pressed.

```
while 1:
    k = pygame.key.get_pressed()
    if k[pygame.K_UP]:
        y-=yChange-=10
    if k[pygame.K_DOWN]:
        y+=yChange+=10
```

16.2.4. Game loops and text

This next script will cover various loops that most pygame tutorials pass up. Nested loops can be quite powerful when utilized correctly. A splash screen is nice to have and the same code could be considered a transition point to another level or scene.

```
#gameloop1.py
import pygame
white=(255,255,255) # RGB values
black=(0,0,0)
green=(0,255,0)
red=(255,0,0)
yellow=(255,255,0)
blue=(0,0,255)
pygame.init()
display=pygame.display.set_mode((800,600))
clock = pygame.time.Clock()
font=pygame.font.SysFont(None,25)
def splash():
    intro=True
    while intro:
        for event in pygame.event.get():
            if event.type==pygame.QUIT:
                pygame.quit()
                quit()
            if event.type==pygame.KEYDOWN:
                if event.key == pygame.K_c:
                    intro=False
                if event.key==pygame.K_q:
                    pygame.quit()
                    quit()
        display.fill(white)
        message("Wellcome!!!", black,300,300 )
        message("Press 'c' to continue or 'q' to Quit",black,300,400)
        pygame.display.update()
        clock.tick(15)
def message(msg,color,posx,posy):
    mytext=font.render(msg,True,color)
    display.blit(mytext,[posx,posy])
```

```
def game():
    exit=False
    over=False
    x=300; y=300
    xChange=0; yChange=0
    while not exit: # exit loop
        while over == True: # over loop
            display.fill(blue)
            message("Game over 'c' to continue 'q' to quit",
yellow, 300,300)
            pygame.display.update()
            for event in pygame.event.get():
                if event.type==pygame.QUIT:
                    over=False
                    exit=True
                if event.type == pygame.KEYDOWN:
                    if event.key == pygame.K_q:
                        exit = True
                        over = False
                    if event.key == pygame.K_c:
                        game()
        for event in pygame.event.get(): # event handling
            if event.type==pygame.QUIT:
                exit=True
            k=pygame.key.get_pressed()
            if k[pygame.K_LEFT]:
                xChange-=10
            elif k[pygame.K_RIGHT]:
                xChange+=10
            elif k[pygame.K_UP]:
                yChange-=10
            elif k[pygame.K_DOWN]:
                yChange+=10
            else:
                xChange=0
```

```
                yChange=0
            if x==700: # borders
                xChange=-10
                yChange=0
            if x==10:
                xChange=10
                yChange=0
            if y==500:
                yChange=-10
                xChange=0
            if y==10:
                over=True
            x += xChange # continue from previous location
            y += yChange
            display.fill(black) # not rendered without update
            message("Move square in any direction...", yellow,
300,50)
            message("Too far up exits loop...", yellow, 300,70)
            pygame.draw.rect(display,white,[x,y,20,20]) # coords,
w,h
            pygame.display.update()
            clock.tick(10)
        pygame.quit()
        quit()
    splash()
    game()
```

A couple of new things have been introduced such as font(), message(), and blit(). Also note that 'x' and 'y' needed to be moved into the main loop for the game.

16.2.5. Images

In this section, we introduce image.load(), and random(). Don't forget the display.update().

```
#image1.py
import pygame
```

Figure 16.3.: Pygame Transition Screens

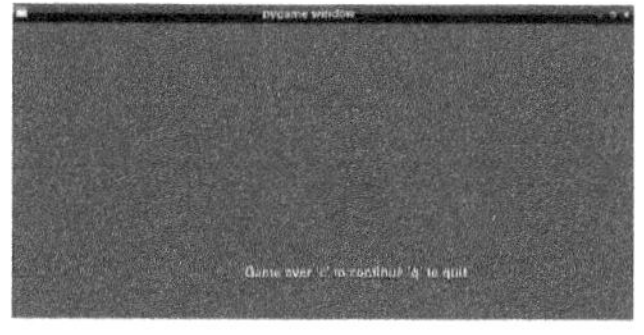

```
import random
white=(255,255,255) # RGB values
black=(0,0,0)
green=(0,255,0)
red=(255,0,0)
yellow=(255,255,0)
blue=(0,0,255)
pygame.init()
display=pygame.display.set_mode((800,600))
clock = pygame.time.Clock()
font=pygame.font.SysFont(None,25)
bg=pygame.image.load("gimpbackground.png")
star=pygame.image.load('assortstar1.png')
def message(msg,color,posx,posy):
    mytext=font.render(msg,True,color)
    display.blit(mytext,[posx,posy])
def game():
    exit=False
    x=300; y=300
    xChange=0; yChange=0
    boxX=round(random.randrange(0,800-10) /10.0) *10.0
    boxY=round(random.randrange(0,600-10) /10.0) *10.0
    while not exit: # exit loop
        for event in pygame.event.get(): # event handling
```

```
        if event.type==pygame.QUIT:
            exit=True
        k=pygame.key.get_pressed()
        if k[pygame.K_LEFT]:
            xChange-=10
        elif k[pygame.K_RIGHT]:
            xChange+=10
        elif k[pygame.K_UP]:
            yChange-=10
        elif k[pygame.K_DOWN]:
            yChange+=10
        else:
            xChange=0
            yChange=0
    if x==700: # borders
        xChange=-10
        yChange=0
    if x==10:
        xChange=10
        yChange=0
    if y==500:
        yChange=-10
        xChange=0
    if y==10:
        exit=True
    x += xChange # continue from previous location
    y += yChange
    display.fill(black) # not rendered without update
    display.blit(bg,(0,0))
    message("Move square in any direction...", yellow,
300,50)
    message("Too far up exits loop...", yellow, 300,70)
    pygame.draw.rect(display,yellow,[boxX,boxY,20,20])
    display.blit(star,[x,y])
    pygame.display.update()
```

```
        clock.tick(10)
    pygame.quit()
    quit()
game()
```

16.2.6. Collision detection

What happens when two blits collide?

```
#collision.py
import pygame
import random
white=(255,255,255) # RGB
values black=(0,0,0)
green=(0,255,0)
red=(255,0,0)
yellow=(255,255,0)
blue=(0,0,255)
pygame.init()
display=pygame.display.set_mode((800,600))
clock = pygame.time.Clock()
font=pygame.font.SysFont(None,25)
bg=pygame.image.load("gimpbackground.png")
star=pygame.image.load('assortstar1.png')
def message(msg,color,posx,posy):
    mytext=font.render(msg,True,color)
    display.blit(mytext,[posx,posy])
def game():
    exit=False
    x=300; y=300
    xChange=0; yChange=0
    boxX=round(random.randrange(0,800-10) /10.0) *10.0
    boxY=round(random.randrange(0,600-10) /10.0) *10.0
    while not exit: # exit loop
        for event in pygame.event.get(): # event handling
            if event.type==pygame.QUIT:
                exit=True
            k=pygame.key.get_pressed()
            if k[pygame.K_LEFT]:
                xChange-=10
            elif k[pygame.K_RIGHT]:
```

```
            xChange+=10
        elif k[pygame.K_UP]:
            yChange-=10
        elif k[pygame.K_DOWN]:
            yChange+=10
        else:
            xChange=0
            yChange=0
    if x==700: # borders
        xChange=-10; yChange=0
    if x==10:
        xChange=10; yChange=0
    if y==500:
        yChange=-10; xChange=0
    if y==10:
        exit=True
    x += xChange # continue from previous location
    y += yChange
    display.blit(bg,(0,0))
    message("Move square in any direction...", yellow,
300,50)
    pygame.draw.rect(display,yellow,[boxX,boxY,40,40])
    display.blit(star,[x,y]) pygame.display.update()
    if x== boxX and y==boxY: #collision
        print("Boom!!!")
        boxX=round(random.randrange(0,800-10) /10.0) *10.0
        boxY=round(random.randrange(0,600-10) /10.0) *10.0
    clock.tick(10)
  pygame.quit()
  quit()
game()
```

16.2.7. Summary parts of a game

1. Initialization

a) screen=pygame.display.set_mode()
b) images=pygame.image.load()
c) clock=pygame.time.Clock()
d) key, mouse etc...
e) misc...

2. Main loop
   a) User Input
      i. managed by clock.tick()
      ii. key events
      iii. screen.fill()
   b) Simulation
      i. speed, forward, reverse, direction
   c) Rendering
      i. rotate()
      ii. get_rect()
      iii. position
      iv. blit()
      v. display.flip()

16.2.8. Game Engine Architecture

In the simplest form, the architecture is the summary at the beginning of the chapter with the following new components.

- Action(run, drive, jump,etc...)
- Input()
- game logic(is, else, etc...)
- camera(update)
- world(update)
- GUI(update)
- Collision(AI)(update)

- Audio()
- Render(draw)

All of this needs to be mapped out in a meshed map where nearly every component interacts with every other component. You should also document each component if you would like to retain some sanity. As you begin to write each component, it becomes a framework class that you use for all your tasks.

Now we prepare to send messages from one component to another component. Create a bus module that each component can reference.

I would start out writing the following classes and encapsulate the components above.

- class Sprite():
  - update(), checkboundry()
- class ComplexSprite():
  - Wrap() #wrap around screen
  - Bounce() #bounce off screen
  - Stop() # stop at edge of screem
  - speed()
  - update()
  - angle()
  - etc...
- class Scene():
  - init()
  - start/stop()
  - mainloop()
  - update()
  - events()
- class Label():

  - init()
  - update()

- class Multilabel():
  - multi(),long(), update()
- class Button():
  - etc...
- class scroller():
  - etc...

16.3. Creating a Game Summary

You want to prototype as many features as you can for your game engine so you can focus more on game logic and less on design. For instance a game will contain multiple "Scene class" instructions, game play, progress, new elements, levels, and restart or end. Eighty percent of the features you prototype into the engine can be reused for other games of the same type, such as "side scroller games" , "platform games" , "top down", and "hybrid games". Though it is a bit of a jump from 2d to 3d games, the concepts are still the same.

17. Stock Market

17.1. Stock Market

I have been using python for stock market analysis for quite some time now with multiple accounts setup with a handful of preferred brokerage firms. Still, irregardless of the services they provide, there is always something that seems to be missing from one brokerage firm to the next.

It is often necessary to grab data from Scottrade™, Etrade™, Marketfy™, Gurufocus™, Google™, Yahoo™, or another service.

Scraping information from these sites is perfectly free, though you will need to register these services for commercial use if you plan on monetizing a feature obtained from those services. Most of those companies get their information from Morningstar.com™ and or Bloomberglabs.com™.

17.1.0.1. Yahoo

query.yahooapis.com The example below uses the query API from yahoo.com and yahoo returns a dictionary result of the data. You can pass in a list of values.

```
#yahooapis
import json
import urllib
from pprint import pprint
base_url = 'https://query.yahooapis.com/v1/public/yql?'
query = {
```

```
        'q': 'select * from yahoo.finance.quote where symbol
    in ("YHOO","AAPL")',
        'format': 'json',
        'env': 'store://datatables.org/alltableswithkeys'
    }
    url = base_url + urllib.urlencode(query)
    response = urllib.urlopen(url)
    data = response.read().decode('utf-8')
    quote = json.loads(data)
    pprint(quote)
    print type(quote)
```

Results:


```
{u'query': {u'count': 2, u'created': u'2017-01-02T21:56:55Z', u'lang':
u'en-US', u'results':

{u'quote': [{u'AverageDailyVolume': u'9973590', u'Change': u'+0.00',
u'DaysHigh': u'39.00',

u'DaysLow': u'38.43', u'DaysRange': u'38.43 - 39.00', u'LastTradePriceOnly':
u'38.67', u'MarketCapitalization':

u'36.90B', u'Name': u'Yahoo! Inc.', u'StockExchange': u'NMS', u'Symbol':
u'YHOO', u'Volume': u'6432792',

u'YearHigh':u'44.92', u'YearLow': u'26.15', u'symbol': u'YHOO'},


{u'AverageDailyVolume': u'32082600', u'Change': u'+0.00', u'DaysHigh':

u'117.20', u'DaysLow': u'115.43', u'DaysRange': u'115.43 - 117.20',
u'LastTradePriceOnly'

: u'115.82', u'MarketCapitalization': u'617.59B', u'Name': u'Apple Inc.',
u'StockExchange':

u'NMS', u'Symbol': u'AAPL', u'Volume': u'30586265', u'YearHigh':
u'118.69', u'YearLow':

u'89.47', u'symbol': u'AAPL'}]}}} <type 'dict'>
```


Historical

Getting historical data can be obtained easily as well. However it can't be more than 18 months. You can easily create a script to process 10 years of data by chaining data from each previous year.

```
#historical.py
import json
import urllib
from pprint import pprint
base_url = 'https://query.yahooapis.com/v1/public/yql?'
query = {
    'q': 'select * from yahoo.finance.historicaldata
    where symbol in ("AAPL") and startDate ="2004-
05-10"
    and endDate="2005-05-10"',
    'format': 'json',
    'env': 'store://datatables.org/alltableswithkeys'
    }
url = base_url + urllib.urlencode(query)
response = urllib.urlopen(url)
data = response.read().decode('utf-8')
quote = json.loads(data)
pprint(quote)
print type(quote)
```

Scraping You can scrape finance.yahoo.com for certain data as well, though it is recommended that you take a look at the data you are scraping. Below are some carefully positioned print statements. While it's always better to leverage an API to get your metrics, sometimes you have to resort to scraping raw information off of a web page. Before you start creating the next script you will need to download 'BeautifulSoup': *pip install BeautifulSoup*

```
#scrape.py
import urllib
from BeautifulSoup import *
symbol="AAPL"
url = "http://finance.yahoo.com/q?s=" + symbol +"&q1=1"
htmlfile = urllib.urlopen(url)
htmltext = htmlfile.read()
#print htmltext
soup = BeautifulSoup(htmltext)
#print soup
table=soup.findAll('td')
for row in table:
    print row.text
```

Results:

```
Search
Previous Close
115.82
Open
116.65
Bid
115.48 x 500
Ask
115.60 x 700
Day&#x27;s Range
115.43 - 117.20
52 Week Range
89.47 - 118.69
Volume
30,586,265
Avg. Volume
32,011,239
Market Cap
617.59B
Beta
1.42
PE Ratio (TTM)
13.94
EPS (TTM)
N/A
Earnings Date
N/A
Dividend &amp; Yield
2.28 (1.97%)
Ex-Dividend Date
N/A
1y Target Est
N/A
```

As you can see from the above example, each table item prints on its own line. In the example below, I'm searching for the EPS of a stock so I can calculate PE ratio based on current stock price and Earnings Per Share (EPS). Notice the EPS has a TTM (Trailing Twelve Months) symbol meaning the EPS is a calculation for the most recent twelve months. Websites change all the time, so scraping code will constantly need to be adjusted in order to extract accurate results.

Create your own dictionary of the values you want using both query API and finance scraping.

```
#eps.py
import json
import urllib
```

```
from pprint import pprint
from BeautifulSoup import *
base_url = 'https://query.yahooapis.com/v1/public/yql?'
def querytool(sql):
    query = {
        'q': sql,
        'format': 'json',
        'env': 'store://datatables.org/alltableswithkeys'
    }
    return query
def getdata(base_url,qtool):
    url = base_url + urllib.urlencode(qtool)
    response = urllib.urlopen(url)
    data = response.read().decode('utf-8')
    quote = json.loads(data)
    return quote
def getEPS(symbol):
    ar=[]
    num=0;token=0
    url = "http://finance.yahoo.com/q?s=" + symbol +"&q1=1"
    htmlfile = urllib.urlopen(url)
    htmltext = htmlfile.read()
    soup = BeautifulSoup(htmltext)
    table=soup.findAll('td')
    for row in table:
        ar.append(row.text)
        num+=1
        if 'P/E' in row.text:
            token=num
    return ar[token]
if __name__=="__main__":
    symbol="AAPL"
    sql='select * from yahoo.finance.quote where symbol
in ("%s")' % symbol
    Q=querytool(sql)
    stock=getdata(base_url,Q) # returns json or nested
dict
```

```
        data=stock['query']['results']['quote'] # relevant stock
    data dictionary
        data['P/E']=getEPS(symbol)
        print data
```

Results:

{u'YearLow': u'89.47', 'P/E': u", u'MarketCapitalization': u'617.59B', u'DaysHigh': u'117.20', u'symbol': u'AAPL', u'DaysLow': u'115.43', u'Volume': u'30586265', u'StockExchange': u'NMS', u'DaysRange': u'115.43 - 117.20', u'AverageDailyVolume': u'32082600', u'LastTradePriceOnly': u'115.82', u'YearHigh': u'118.69', u'Symbol': u'AAPL', u'Change': u'+0.00', u'Name': u'Apple Inc.'}

CSV chartapi.finance.yahoo.com generates a CSV file you can download and parse. You can also extract 'intradata' metrics as well and save the results output in a text file called AAPL.txt that can be used in chart.py later.

```
# script to grab stock data
#csvdata.py
import urllib
import time
import datetime
stockpull='AAPL' # this can be a list to loop through
def MyStock(stock):
    print "Get stock data", stock
    print str(datetime.datetime.fromtimestamp(time.time()).strftime('%y-
%m-%d %H:%M:%S'))
    url="http://chartapi.finance.yahoo.com/instrument/1.0/"+
stock+"/chartdata;type=quote;range=1y/csv"
    #url="http://chartapi.finance.yahoo.com/instrument/1.0/"+
stock+"/chartdata;type=quote;range=10d/csv"
    #url="http://chartapi.finance.yahoo.com/instrument/1.0/"+
stock+"/chartdata;type=quote;range=1d/csv"
    response=urllib.urlopen(url)
    html=response.read()
    print html
MyStock(stockpull)
```

The results produce time stamp, high, low, open, and volume:

```
20160929,112.1800,113.8000,111.8000,113.1600,35887000
20160930,113.0500,113.3700,111.8000,112.4600,36379100
20161003,112.5200,113.0500,112.2800,112.7100,21701800
20161004,113.0000,114.3100,112.6300,113.0600,29736800
```

```
20161005,113.0500,113.6600,112.6900,113.4000,21453100
20161006,113.8900,114.3400,113.1300,113.7000,28779300
20161007,114.0600,114.5600,113.5100,114.3100,24358400
20161010,116.0500,116.7500,114.7200,115.0200,36236000
```

The type of 'URL' you choose will determine the type of data received. '1y' equals a year average. '10d' equals '5' min average.

```
1483112641,116.1700,116.2700,116.1600,116.2000,177700
1483112940,116.0800,116.1700,116.0500,116.1602,276500
1483113240,116.0600,116.1400,116.0400,116.0850,226500
1483113540,116.2094,116.2300,116.0600,116.0700,222600
1483113841,116.2400,116.2500,116.1700,116.2000,180900
1483114140,116.2299,116.2500,116.1835,116.2403,119900
1483114440,116.1800,116.2600,116.1700,116.2250,166200
1483114740,116.2850,116.3000,116.1899,116.1899,152600
```

You can extract time and date as follows:

```
>>> import calendar
>>> time.gmtime(1483131600)
time.struct_time(tm_year=2016, tm_mon=12, tm_mday=30, tm_hour=21,
tm_min=0, tm_sec=0, tm_wday=4, tm_yday=365, tm_isdst=0)
>>>
```

Graphics You can use Matplotlib to graph your results if you save it to file. You will need to convert intra-data epoch time to standard date format.

Get stock data:

```
#chart.py
import time
import datetime
import numpy as np
import matplotlib.pyplot as plt
import matplotlib.ticker as mticker
import matplotlib.dates as mdates
mystock='AAPL'
def gData(stock):
    stockFile=stock+".txt"
    date,closep,highp,lowp,openp,volume= np.loadtxt
(stockFile,delimiter=',',unpack=True,
converters={0: mdates.strpdate2num('%Y%m%d')})
```

```
        fig=plt.figure()
        ax1=plt.subplot(1,1,1) # how much by how much by
        ax1.plot(date,openp)
        ax1.plot(date,highp)
        ax1.plot(date,lowp)
        ax1.plot(date,closep)
        ax1.xaxis.set_major_locator(mticker.MaxNLocator(10))
#max10days
        ax1.xaxis.set_major_formatter(mdates.DateFormatter('%Y-
%m-%d'))
        for label in ax1.xaxis.get_ticklabels():
            label.set_rotation(45)
        plt.show()
    gData(mystock)
```

Figure 17.1.: Matplot Graph

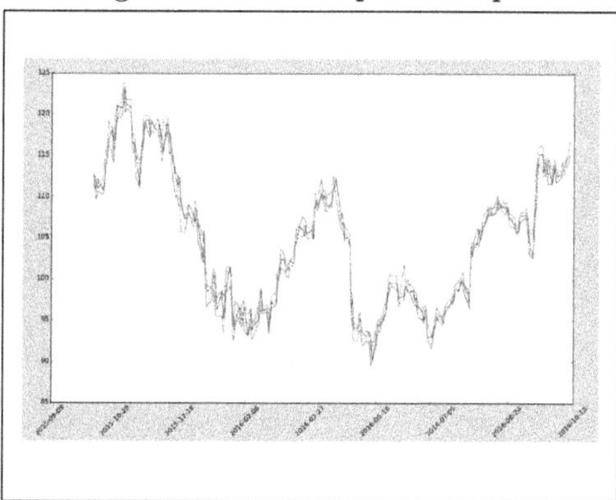

Matplotlib is an extremely powerful tool and has the ability to do candlestick charts and various other charts. However if you plan on putting this on the web Javascript might work better for real time charting. Morningstar.com and Bloomberg both provide API's for metrics and analysis.

18. Closing Thoughts

18.1. Closing Thoughts

As the title suggests, this is rapid programming. Your ultimate goal is to use python to create programs or applications that are either free, for sale or just fun. Programming allows you to automate repetitive tasks freeing you to focus on other things.

Most authors expect you to read every word in the book. While this works for some, I know it's possible you're not going to do that. Chances are you skipped a lot just to get here. Hopefully, you have written at least a few lines of code. It is my goal that this book is flexible enough to appeal to beginner and experienced programmers alike. It is filled with delicious reusable morsels of code that are also available on my GitHub. Software engineering is complex system made up of simple programs that when put together make amazing and fun things possible.

If you do use any of the code from the book, please take a minute to send me a message and let me know what you think!

See you in cyberspace.

Part III.

Appendixes

Appendix A

Python Card uses OSI BSD Licensing:

Open Source Initiative OSI - The BSD License:Licensing

The BSD License

The following is a BSD license template. To generate your own license, change the values of OWNER, ORGANIZATION and YEAR from their original values as given here, and substitute your own.

Note: You may optionally omit clause 3 and still be OSD-conformant. On January 9th, 2008 the OSI Board approved the "Simplified BSD License" variant used by FreeBSD and others, which omits the final "no-endorsement" clause and is thus roughly equivalent to the MIT License.

Historical Note: The original license used on BSD Unix had four clauses. The advertising clause (the third of four clauses) required you to acknowledge use of U.C. Berkeley code in your advertising of any product using that code. It was officially rescinded by the Director of the Office of Technology Licensing of the University of California on July 22nd, 1999. He states that clause 3 is "hereby deleted in its entirety." The four clause license has not been approved by OSI. The license below does not contain the advertising clause.

This prelude is not part of the license.

<OWNER> = Regents of the University of California <ORGANIZATION> = University of California, Berkeley

<YEAR> = 1998

In the original BSD license, both occurrences of the phrase "COPYRIGHT HOLDERS AND CONTRIBUTORS" in the disclaimer read "REGENTS AND CONTRIBUTORS".

Here is the license template:

Copyright (c) <YEAR>, <OWNER>

All rights reserved.

Redistribution and use in source and binary forms, with or without modification, are permitted provided that the following conditions are met:

Redistributions of source code must retain the above copyright notice, this list of conditions and the following disclaimer.

Redistributions in binary form must reproduce the above copyright notice, this list of conditions and the following disclaimer in the documentation and/or other materials provided with the distribution.

Neither the name of the <ORGANIZATION> nor the names of its contributors may be used to endorse or promote products derived from this software without specific prior written permission.

THIS SOFTWARE IS PROVIDED BY THE COPYRIGHT HOLDERS AND CONTRIBUTORS "AS IS" AND ANY EXPRESS OR IMPLIED WARRANTIES, INCLUDING, BUT NOT LIMITED TO, THE IMPLIED WARRANTIES OF MERCHANTABILITY AND FITNESS FOR A PARTICULAR PURPOSE ARE DISCLAIMED. IN NO EVENT SHALL THE COPYRIGHT HOLDER OR CONTRIBUTORS BE LIABLE FOR ANY DIRECT, INDIRECT, INCIDENTAL, SPECIAL, EXEMPLARY, OR CONSEQUENTIAL DAMAGES (INCLUDING, BUT NOT LIMITED TO, PROCUREMENT OF SUBSTITUTE GOODS OR SERVICES; LOSS OF USE, DATA, OR PROFITS; OR BUSINESS INTERRUPTION) HOWEVER CAUSED AND ON ANY THEORY OF LIABILITY, WHETHER IN CONTRACT, STRICT LIABILITY, OR TORT (INCLUDING NEGLIGENCE OR OTHERWISE) ARISING IN ANY WAY OUT OF THE USE OF THIS SOFTWARE, EVEN IF ADVISED OF THE POSSIBILITY OF SUCH DAMAGE.

Appendix B

Pygame uses LGPL Licensing:

GNU LESSER GENERAL PUBLIC LICENSE
Version 2.1, February 1999

[This is the first released version of the Lesser GPL. It also counts as the successor of the GNU Library Public License, version 2, hence the version number 2.1.]

Preamble

The licenses for most software are designed to take away your freedom to share and change it. By contrast, the GNU General Public Licenses are intended to guarantee your freedom to share and change free software–to make sure the software is free for all its users.

This license, the Lesser General Public License, applies to some specially designated software packages–typically libraries–of the Free Software Foundation and other authors who decide to use it. You can use it too, but we suggest you first think carefully about whether this license or the ordinary General Public License is the better strategy to use in any particular case, based on the explanations below.

When we speak of free software, we are referring to freedom of use, not price. Our General Public Licenses are designed to make sure that you have the freedom to distribute copies of free software (and charge for this service if you wish); that you receive source code or can get it if you want it; that you can change the software and use pieces of it in new free programs; and that you are informed that you can do these things.

To protect your rights, we need to make restrictions that forbid distributors to deny you these rights or to ask you to surrender these rights. These restrictions translate to certain responsibilities for you if you distribute copies of the library or if you modify it.

For example, if you distribute copies of the library, whether gratis or for a fee, you must give the recipients all the rights that we gave you. You must make sure that they, too, receive or can get the source code. If you link other code with the library, you must provide complete object files to the recipients, so that they can relink them with the library after making changes to the library and recompiling it. And you must show them these terms so they know their rights.

We protect your rights with a two-step method: (1) we copyright the library, and (2) we offer you this license, which gives you legal permission to copy, distribute and/or modify the library.

To protect each distributor, we want to make it very clear that there is no warranty for the free library. Also, if the library is modified by someone else and passed on, the recipients should know that what they have is not the original version, so that the original author's reputation will not be affected by problems that might be introduced by others.

Finally, software patents pose a constant threat to the existence of any free program. We wish to make sure that a company cannot effectively restrict the users of a free program by obtaining a restrictive license from a patent holder. Therefore, we insist that any patent license obtained for a version of the library must be consistent with the full freedom of use specified in this license.

Most GNU software, including some libraries, is covered by the ordinary GNU General Public License. This license, the GNU Lesser General Public License, applies to certain designated libraries, and is quite different from the ordinary General Public License. We use this license for certain libraries in order to permit linking those libraries into non-free programs.

When a program is linked with a library, whether statically or using a shared library, the combination of the two is legally speaking a combined work, a derivative of the original library. The ordinary General Public License therefore permits such linking only if the entire combination fits its criteria of freedom. The Lesser General Public License permits more lax criteria for linking other code with the library.

We call this license the "Lesser" General Public License because it does Less to protect the user's freedom than the ordinary General Public License. It also provides other free software developers Less of an advantage over competing non-free programs. These disadvantages are the reason we use the ordinary General Public License for many libraries. However, the Lesser license provides advantages in certain special circumstances.

For example, on rare occasions, there may be a special need to encourage the widest possible use of a certain library, so that it becomes a de-facto standard. To achieve this, non-free programs must be allowed to use the library. A more frequent case is that a free library does the same job as widely used non-free libraries. In this case, there is little to gain by limiting the free library to free software only, so we use the Lesser General Public License.

In other cases, permission to use a particular library in non-free programs enables a greater number of people to use a large body of free software. For example, permission to use the GNU C Library in non-free programs enables many more people to use the whole GNU operating system, as well as its variant, the GNU/Linux operating system.

Although the Lesser General Public License is Less protective of the users' freedom, it does ensure that the user of a program that is linked with the Library has the freedom and the wherewithal to run that program using a modified version of the Library.

The precise terms and conditions for copying, distribution and modification follow. Pay close attention to the difference between a "work based on the library" and a "work that uses the library". The former contains code derived from the library, whereas the latter must be combined with the library in order to run.

GNU LESSER GENERAL PUBLIC LICENSE TERMS AND CONDITIONS FOR COPYING, DISTRIBUTION AND MODIFICATION

0. This License Agreement applies to any software library or other program which contains a notice placed by the copyright holder or other authorized party saying it may be distributed under the terms of this Lesser General Public License (also called "this License"). Each licensee is addressed as "you". A "library" means a collection of software functions and/or data prepared so as to be conveniently linked with application programs (which use some of those functions and data) to form executables. The "Library", below, refers to any such software library or work which has been distributed under these terms. A "work based on the Library" means either the Library or any derivative work under copyright law: that is to say, a work containing the Library or a portion of it, either verbatim or with modifications and/or translated straightforwardly into another language. (Hereinafter, translation is included without limitation in the term "modification".) "Source code" for a work means the preferred form of the work for making modifications to it. For a library, complete source code means all the source code for all modules it contains, plus any associated interface definition files, plus the scripts used to control compilation and installation of the library. Activities other than copying, distribution and modification are not covered by this License; they are outside its scope. The act of running a program using the Library is not restricted, and output from such a program is covered only if its contents constitute a work based on the Library (independent of the use of the Library in a tool for writing it). Whether that is true depends on what the Library does and what the program that uses the Library does.

1. You may copy and distribute verbatim copies of the Library's complete source code as you receive it, in any medium, provided that you conspicuously and appropriately publish on each copy an appropriate copyright notice and disclaimer of warranty; keep intact all the notices that refer to this License and to the absence of any warranty; and distribute a copy of this License along with the Library. **You may charge a fee for the physical act of transferring a copy, and you may at your option offer warranty protection in exchange for a fee.**

2. You may modify your copy or copies of the Library or any portion of it, thus forming a work based on the Library, and copy and distribute such modifications or work under the terms of Section 1 above, provided that you also meet all of these conditions:

a) The modified work must itself be a software library.

b) You must cause the files modified to carry prominent notices stating that you changed the files and the date of any change.

c) You must cause the whole of the work to be licensed at no charge to all third parties under the terms of this License.

d) If a facility in the modified Library refers to a function or a table of data to be supplied by an application program that uses the facility, other than as an argument passed when the facility is invoked, then you must make a good faith effort to ensure that, in the event an application does not supply such function or table, the facility still operates, and performs whatever part of its purpose remains meaningful. (For example, a function in a library to compute square roots has a purpose that is entirely well-defined independent of the application. Therefore, Subsection 2d requires that any application-supplied function or table used by this function must be optional: if the application does not supply it, the square root function must still compute square roots.) These requirements apply to the modified work as a whole. If identifiable sections of that work are not derived from the Library, and can be reasonably considered independent and separate works in themselves, then this License, and its terms, do not apply to those sections when you distribute them as separate works. But when you distribute the same sections as part of a whole which is a work based on the Library, the distribution of the whole must be on the terms of this License, whose permissions for other licensees extend to the entire whole, and thus to each and every part regardless of who wrote it. Thus, it is not the intent of this section to claim rights or contest your rights to work written entirely by you; rather, the intent is to exercise the right to control the distribution of derivative or collective works based on the Library. In addition, mere aggregation of another work not based on the Library with the Library (or with a work based on the Library) on a volume of a storage or distribution medium does not bring the other work under the scope of this License.

3. You may opt to apply the terms of the ordinary GNU General Public License instead of this License to a given copy of the Library. To do this, you must alter all the notices that refer to this License, so that they refer to the ordinary GNU General Public License, version 2, instead of to this License. (If a newer version than version 2 of the ordinary GNU General Public License has appeared, then you can specify that version instead if you wish.) Do not make any other change in these notices. Once this change is made in a given copy, it is irreversible for that copy, so the ordinary GNU General Public License applies to all subsequent copies and derivative works made from that copy. This option is useful when you wish to copy part of the code of the Library into a program that is not a library.

4. You may copy and distribute the Library (or a portion or derivative of it, under Section 2) in object code or executable form under the terms of Sections 1 and 2 above provided that you accompany it with the complete corresponding machine-readable source code, which must be distributed under the terms of Sections 1 and 2 above on a medium customarily used for software interchange. If distribution of object code is made by offering access to copy from a designated place, then offering equivalent access to copy the source code from the same place satisfies the requirement to distribute the source code, even though third parties are not compelled to copy the source along with the object code.

5. A program that contains no derivative of any portion of the Library, but is designed to work with the Library by being compiled or linked with it, is called a "work that uses the Library". Such a work, in isolation, is not a derivative work of the Library, and therefore falls outside the scope of this License. However, linking a "work that uses the Library" with the Library creates an executable that is a derivative of the Library (because it contains portions of the Library), rather than a "work that uses the library". The executable is therefore covered by this License. Section 6 states terms for distribution of such executables. When a "work that uses the Library" uses material from a header file that is part of the Library, the object code for the work may be a derivative work of the Library even though the source code is not. Whether this is true is especially significant if the work can be linked without the Library, or if the work is itself a library. The threshold for this to be true is not precisely defined by law. If such an object file uses only numerical parameters, data structure layouts and accessors, and small macros and small inline functions (ten lines or less in length), then the use of the object file is unrestricted, regardless of whether it is legally a derivative work. (Executables containing this object code plus portions of the Library will still fall under Section 6.) Otherwise, if the work is a derivative of the Library, you may distribute the object code for the work under the terms of Section 6. Any executables containing that work also fall under Section 6, whether or not they are linked directly with the Library itself.

6. As an exception to the Sections above, you may also combine or link a "work that uses the Library" with the Library to produce a work containing portions of the Library, and distribute that work under terms of your choice, provided that the terms permit modification of the work for the customer's own use and reverse engineering for debugging such modifications. You must

give prominent notice with each copy of the work that the Library is used in it and that the Library and its use are covered by this License. You must supply a copy of this License. If the work during execution displays copyright notices, you must include the copyright notice for the Library among them, as well as a reference directing the user to the copy of this License. Also, you must do one of these things:

a) Accompany the work with the complete corresponding machine-readable source code for the Library including whatever changes were used in the work (which must be distributed under Sections 1 and 2 above); and, if the work is an executable linked with the Library, with the complete machine-readable "work that uses the Library", as object code and/or source code, so that the user can modify the Library and then relink to produce a modified executable containing the modified Library. (It is understood that the user who changes the contents of definitions files in the Library will not necessarily be able to recompile the application to use the modified definitions.)

b) Use a suitable shared library mechanism for linking with the Library. A suitable mechanism is one that (1) uses at run time a copy of the library already present on the user's computer system, rather than copying library functions into the executable, and (2) will operate properly with a modified version of the library, if the user installs one, as long as the modified version is interface-compatible with the version that the work was made with.

c) Accompany the work with a written offer, valid for at least three years, to give the same user the materials specified in Subsection 6a, above, for a charge no more than the cost of performing this distribution.

d) If distribution of the work is made by offering access to copy from a designated place, offer equivalent access to copy the above specified materials from the same place.

e) Verify that the user has already received a copy of these materials or that you have already sent this user a copy. For an executable, the required form of the "work that uses the Library" must include any data and utility programs needed for reproducing the executable from it. However, as a special exception, the materials to be distributed need not include anything that is normally distributed (in either source or binary form) with the major components (compiler, kernel, and so on) of the operating system on which the executable runs, unless that component itself accompanies the executable. It may happen that this requirement contradicts the license restrictions of other proprietary libraries that do not normally accompany the operating system. Such a contradiction means you cannot use both them and the Library together in an executable that you distribute.

7. You may place library facilities that are a work based on the Library side-by-side in a single library together with other library facilities not covered by this License, and distribute such a combined library, provided that the separate distribution of the work based on the Library and of the other library facilities is otherwise permitted, and provided that you do these two things:

a) Accompany the combined library with a copy of the same work based on the Library, uncombined with any other library facilities. This must be distributed under the terms of the Sections above.

b) Give prominent notice with the combined library of the fact that part of it is a work based on the Library, and explaining where to find the accompanying uncombined form of the same work.

8. You may not copy, modify, sublicense, link with, or distribute the Library except as expressly provided under this License. Any attempt otherwise to copy, modify, sublicense, link with, or distribute the Library is void, and will automatically terminate your rights under this License. However, parties who have received copies, or rights, from you under this License will not have their licenses terminated so long as such parties remain in full compliance.

9. You are not required to accept this License, since you have not signed it. However, nothing else grants you permission to modify or distribute the Library or its derivative works. These actions are prohibited by law if you do not accept this License. Therefore, by modifying or distributing the Library (or any work based on the Library), you indicate your acceptance of this License to do so, and all its terms and conditions for copying, distributing or modifying the Library or works based on it.

10. Each time you redistribute the Library (or any work based on the Library), the recipient automatically receives a license from the original licensor to copy, distribute, link with or modify the Library subject to these terms and conditions. You may not impose any further restrictions on the recipients' exercise of the rights granted herein. You are not responsible for enforcing compliance by third parties with this License.

11. If, as a consequence of a court judgment or allegation of patent infringement or for any other reason (not limited to patent issues), conditions are imposed on you

(whether by court order, agreement or otherwise) that contradict the conditions of this License, they do not excuse you from the conditions of this License. If you cannot distribute so as to satisfy simultaneously your obligations under this License and any other pertinent obligations, then as a consequence you may not distribute the Library at all. For example, if a patent license would not permit royalty-free redistribution of the Library by all those who receive copies directly or indirectly through you, then the only way you could satisfy both it and this License would be to refrain entirely from distribution of the Library. If any portion of this section is held invalid or unenforceable under any particular circumstance, the balance of the section is intended to apply, and the section as a whole is intended to apply in other circumstances. It is not the purpose of this section to induce you to infringe any patents or other property right claims or to contest validity of any such claims; this section has the sole purpose of protecting the integrity of the free software distribution system which is implemented by public license practices. Many people have made generous contributions to the wide range of software distributed through that system in reliance on consistent application of that system; it is up to the author/donor to decide if he or she is willing to distribute software through any other system and a licensee cannot impose that choice. This section is intended to make thoroughly clear what is believed to be a consequence of the rest of this License.

12. If the distribution and/or use of the Library is restricted in certain countries either by patents or by copyrighted interfaces, the original copyright holder who places the Library under this License may add an explicit geographical distribution limitation excluding those countries, so that distribution is permitted only in or among countries not thus excluded. In such case, this License incorporates the limitation as if written in the body of this License.

13. The Free Software Foundation may publish revised and/or new versions of the Lesser General Public License from time to time. Such new versions will be similar in spirit to the present version, but may differ in detail to address new problems or concerns. Each version is given a distinguishing version number. If the Library specifies a version number of this License which applies to it and "any later version", you have the option of following the terms and conditions either of that version or of any later version published by the Free Software Foundation. If the Library does not specify a license version number, you may choose any version ever published by the Free Software Foundation.

14. If you wish to incorporate parts of the Library into other free programs whose distribution conditions are incompatible with these, write to the author to ask for permission. For software which is copyrighted by the Free Software Foundation, write to the Free Software Foundation; we sometimes make exceptions for this. Our decision will be guided by the two goals of preserving the free status of all derivatives of our free software and of promoting the sharing and reuse of software generally.

NO WARRANTY

15. BECAUSE THE LIBRARY IS LICENSED FREE OF CHARGE, THERE IS NO WARRANTY FOR THE LIBRARY, TO THE EXTENT PERMITTED BY APPLICABLE LAW. EXCEPT WHEN OTHERWISE STATED IN WRITING THE COPYRIGHT HOLDERS AND/OR OTHER PARTIES PROVIDE THE LIBRARY "AS IS" WITHOUT WARRANTY OF ANY KIND, EITHER EXPRESSED OR IMPLIED, INCLUDING, BUT NOT LIMITED TO, THE IMPLIED WARRANTIES OF MERCHANTABILITY AND FITNESS FOR A PARTICU-

LAR PURPOSE. THE ENTIRE RISK AS TO THE QUALITY AND PERFORMANCE OF THE LIBRARY IS WITH YOU. SHOULD THE LIBRARY PROVE DEFECTIVE, YOU ASSUME THE COST OF ALL NECESSARY SERVICING, REPAIR OR CORRECTION.

16. IN NO EVENT UNLESS REQUIRED BY APPLICABLE LAW OR AGREED TO IN WRITING WILL ANY COPYRIGHT HOLDER, OR ANY OTHER PARTY WHO MAY MODIFY AND/OR REDISTRIBUTE THE LIBRARY AS PERMITTED ABOVE, BE LIABLE TO YOU FOR DAMAGES, INCLUDING ANY GENERAL, SPECIAL, INCIDENTAL OR CONSEQUENTIAL DAMAGES ARISING OUT OF THE USE OR INABILITY TO USE THE LIBRARY (INCLUDING BUT NOT LIMITED TO LOSS OF DATA OR DATA BEING RENDERED INACCURATE OR LOSSES SUSTAINED BY YOU OR THIRD PARTIES OR A FAILURE OF THE LIBRARY TO OPERATE WITH ANY OTHER SOFTWARE), EVEN IF SUCH HOLDER OR OTHER PARTY HAS BEEN ADVISED OF THE POSSIBILITY OF SUCH DAMAGES.

END OF TERMS AND CONDITIONS

How to Apply These Terms to Your New Libraries

If you develop a new library, and you want it to be of the greatest possible use to the public, we recommend making it free software that everyone can redistribute and change. You can do so by permitting redistribution under these terms (or, alternatively, under the terms of the ordinary General Public License).

To apply these terms, attach the following notices to the library. It is safest to attach them to the start of each source file to most effectively convey the exclusion of warranty; and each file should have at least the "copyright" line and a pointer to where the full notice is found.

> <one line to give the library's name and a brief idea of what it does.> Copyright (C) <year> <name of author>
>
> This library is free software; you can redistribute it and/or modify it under the terms of the GNU Lesser General Public License as published by the Free Software Foundation; either version 2.1 of the License, or (at your option) any later version.
>
> This library is distributed in the hope that it will be useful, but WITHOUT ANY WARRANTY; without even the implied warranty of MERCHANTABILITY or FITNESS FOR A PARTICULAR PURPOSE. See the GNU Lesser General Public License for more details.
>
> You should have received a copy of the GNU Lesser General Public License along with this library; if not, write to the Free Software Foundation, Inc., 59 Temple Place, Suite 330, Boston, MA 02111-1307 USA

Also add information on how to contact you by electronic and paper mail.

You should also get your employer (if you work as a programmer) or your school, if any, to sign a "copyright disclaimer" for the library, if necessary. Here is a sample; alter the names:

> Yoyodyne, Inc., hereby disclaims all copyright interest in the library 'Frob' (a library for tweaking knobs) written by James Random Hacker.
>
> <signature of Ty Coon>, 1 April 1990 Ty Coon, President of Vice

That's all there is to it!

Appendix C

Appendix C

Python uses the following license.

PSF LICENSE AGREEMENT FOR PYTHON 2.7.1

1. This LICENSE AGREEMENT is between the Python Software Foundation ("PSF"), and the Individual or Organization ("Licensee") accessing and otherwise using Python 2.7.1 software in source or binary form and its associated documentation.

2. Subject to the terms and conditions of this License Agreement, PSF hereby grants Licensee a nonexclusive, royalty-free, world-wide license to reproduce, analyze, test, perform and/or display publicly, prepare derivative works, distribute, and otherwise use Python 2.7.1 alone or in any derivative version, provided, however, that PSF's License Agreement and PSF's notice of copyright, i.e., "Copyright © 2001-2010 Python Software Foundation; All Rights Reserved" are retained in Python 2.7.1 alone or in any derivative version prepared by Licensee.

3. In the event Licensee prepares a derivative work that is based on or incorporates Python 2.7.1 or any part thereof, and wants to make the derivative work available to others as provided herein, then Licensee hereby agrees to include in any such work a brief summary of the changes made to Python 2.7.1.

4. PSF is making Python 2.7.1 available to Licensee on an "AS IS" basis. PSF MAKES NO REPRESENTATIONS OR WARRANTIES, EXPRESS OR IMPLIED. BY WAY OF EXAMPLE, BUT NOT LIMITATION, PSF MAKES NO AND DISCLAIMS ANY REPRESENTATION OR WARRANTY OF MERCHANTABILITY OR FITNESS FOR ANY PARTICULAR PURPOSE OR THAT THE USE OF PYTHON 2.7.1 WILL NOT INFRINGE ANY THIRD PARTY RIGHTS.

5. PSF SHALL NOT BE LIABLE TO LICENSEE OR ANY OTHER USERS OF PYTHON 2.7.1 FOR ANY INCIDENTAL, SPECIAL, OR CONSEQUENTIAL DAMAGES OR LOSS AS A RESULT OF MODIFYING, DISTRIBUTING, OR OTHERWISE USING PYTHON 2.7.1, OR ANY DERIVATIVE THEREOF, EVEN IF ADVISED OF THE POSSIBILITY THEREOF.

6. This License Agreement will automatically terminate upon a material breach of its terms and conditions.

7. Nothing in this License Agreement shall be deemed to create any relationship of agency, partnership, or joint venture between PSF and Licensee. This License Agreement does not grant permission to use PSF trademarks or trade name in a trademark sense to endorse or promote products or services of Licensee, or any third party.

8. By copying, installing or otherwise using Python 2.7.1, Licensee agrees to be bound by the terms and conditions of this License Agreement.

BEOPEN.COM LICENSE AGREEMENT FOR PYTHON 2.x

BEOPEN PYTHON OPEN SOURCE LICENSE AGREEMENT VERSION 1

1. This LICENSE AGREEMENT is between BeOpen.com ("BeOpen"), having an office at 160 Saratoga Avenue, Santa

Clara, CA 95051, and the Individual or Organization ("Licensee") accessing and otherwise using this software in source or binary form and its associated documentation ("the Software").

2. Subject to the terms and conditions of this BeOpen Python License Agreement, BeOpen hereby grants Licensee a non-exclusive, royalty-free, world-wide license to reproduce, analyze, test, perform and/or display publicly, prepare derivative works, distribute, and otherwise use the Software alone or in any derivative version, provided, however, that the BeOpen Python License is retained in the Software, alone or in any derivative version prepared by Licensee.

3. BeOpen is making the Software available to Licensee on an "AS IS" basis. BEOPEN MAKES NO REPRESENTATIONS OR WARRANTIES, EXPRESS OR IMPLIED. BY WAY OF EXAMPLE, BUT NOT LIMITATION, BEOPEN MAKES NO AND DISCLAIMS ANY REPRESENTATION OR WARRANTY OF MERCHANTABILITY OR FITNESS FOR ANY PARTICULAR PURPOSE OR THAT THE USE OF THE SOFTWARE WILL NOT INFRINGE ANY THIRD PARTY RIGHTS.

4. BEOPEN SHALL NOT BE LIABLE TO LICENSEE OR ANY OTHER USERS OF THE SOFTWARE FOR ANY INCIDENTAL, SPECIAL, OR CONSEQUENTIAL DAMAGES OR LOSS AS A RESULT OF USING, MODIFYING OR DISTRIBUTING THE SOFTWARE, OR ANY DERIVATIVE THEREOF, EVEN IF ADVISED OF THE POSSIBILITY THEREOF.

5. This License Agreement will automatically terminate upon a material breach of its terms and conditions.

6. This License Agreement shall be governed by and interpreted in all respects by the law of the State of California, excluding conflict of law provisions. Nothing in this License Agreement shall be deemed to create any relationship of agency, partnership, or joint venture between BeOpen and

Licensee. This License Agreement does not grant permission to use BeOpen trademarks or trade names in a trademark sense to endorse or promote products or services of Licensee, or any third party. As an exception, the "BeOpen Python" logos available at http://www.pythonlabs.com/logos.html may be used according to the permissions granted on that web page.

7. By copying, installing or otherwise using the software, Licensee agrees to be bound by the terms and conditions of this License Agreement.

CNRI LICENSE AGREEMENT FOR PYTHON 1.6.1

1. This LICENSE AGREEMENT is between the Corporation for National Research Initiatives, having an office at 1895 Preston White Drive, Reston, VA 20191 ("CNRI"), and the Individual or Organization ("Licensee") accessing and otherwise using Python 1.6.1 software in source or binary form and its associated documentation.

2. Subject to the terms and conditions of this License Agreement, CNRI hereby grants Licensee a nonexclusive, royalty-free, world-wide license to reproduce, analyze, test, perform and/or display publicly, prepare derivative works, distribute, and otherwise use Python 1.6.1 alone or in any derivative version, provided, however, that CNRI's License Agreement and CNRI's notice of copyright, i.e., "Copyright © 1995-2001 Corporation for National Research Initiatives; All Rights Reserved" are retained in Python 1.6.1 alone or in any derivative version prepared by Licensee. Alternately, in lieu of CNRI's License Agreement, Licensee may substitute the following text (omitting the quotes): "Python 1.6.1 is made available subject to the terms and conditions in CNRI's License Agreement. This Agreement together with Python 1.6.1 may be located on the Internet using the following unique, persistent identifier (known as a handle): 1895.22/1013. This Agreement may also be obtained from a proxy server on the Internet

using the following URL: http://hdl.handle.net/1895.22/1013."

3. In the event Licensee prepares a derivative work that is based on or incorporates Python 1.6.1 or any part thereof, and wants to make the derivative work available to others as provided herein, then Licensee hereby agrees to include in any such work a brief summary of the changes made to Python 1.6.1.

4. CNRI is making Python 1.6.1 available to Licensee on an "AS IS" basis. CNRI MAKES NO REPRESENTATIONS OR WARRANTIES, EXPRESS OR IMPLIED. BY WAY OF EXAMPLE, BUT NOT LIMITATION, CNRI MAKES NO AND DISCLAIMS ANY REPRESENTATION OR WARRANTY OF MERCHANTABILITY OR FITNESS FOR ANY PARTICULAR PURPOSE OR THAT THE USE OF PYTHON 1.6.1 WILL NOT INFRINGE ANY THIRD PARTY RIGHTS.

5. CNRI SHALL NOT BE LIABLE TO LICENSEE OR ANY OTHER USERS OF PYTHON 1.6.1 FOR ANY INCIDENTAL, SPECIAL, OR CONSEQUENTIAL DAMAGES OR LOSS AS A RESULT OF MODIFYING, DISTRIBUTING, OR OTHERWISE USING PYTHON 1.6.1, OR ANY DERIVATIVE THEREOF, EVEN IF ADVISED OF THE POSSIBILITY THEREOF.

6. This License Agreement will automatically terminate upon a material breach of its terms and conditions.

7. This License Agreement shall be governed by the federal intellectual property law of the United States, including without limitation the federal copyright law, and, to the extent such U.S. federal law does not apply, by the law of the Commonwealth of Virginia, excluding Virginia's conflict of law provisions. Notwithstanding the foregoing, with regard to derivative works based on Python 1.6.1 that incorporate non-separable material that was previously distributed under the GNU General Public License (GPL), the law of the Commonwealth of Virginia shall govern this License Agreement only as to issues arising under or with respect to Paragraphs

4, 5, and 7 of this License Agreement. Nothing in this License Agreement shall be deemed to create any relationship of agency, partnership, or joint venture between CNRI and Licensee. This License Agreement does not grant permission to use CNRI trademarks or trade name in a trademark sense to endorse or promote products or services of Licensee, or any third party.

8. By clicking on the "ACCEPT" button where indicated, or by copying, installing or otherwise using Python 1.6.1, Licensee agrees to be bound by the terms and conditions of this License Agreement.

ACCEPT

CWI LICENSE AGREEMENT FOR PYTHON 0.9.0 THROUGH 1.2

Copyright © 1991 - 1995, Stichting Mathematisch Centrum Amsterdam, The Netherlands. All rights reserved.

Permission to use, copy, modify, and distribute this software and its documentation for any purpose and without fee is hereby granted, provided that the above copyright notice appear in all copies and that both that copyright notice and this permission notice appear in supporting documentation, and that the name of Stichting Mathematisch Centrum or CWI not be used in advertising or publicity pertaining to distribution of the software without specific, written prior permission.

Index

Index

www.ingramcontent.com/pod-product-compliance
Lightning Source LLC
Chambersburg PA
CBHW071106050326
40690CB00008B/1129